MEMO
POLITICAL
OBSERVATIONS OF A
MIDWESTERN
W.A.S.P.

A View from Flyover Country

MICHAEL A. SULLENGER

ISBN 978-1-0980-0980-9 (paperback)
ISBN 978-1-0980-0981-6 (digital)

Christian Faith Publishing, Inc.
832 Park Avenue
Meadville, PA 16335
www.christianfaithpublishing.com

Printed in the United States of America

To Pat and the 700 Club Staff.

Please accept this book and its message with my thanks and gratitude for the blessings you and your program have been to so many over the years. May God continue to bless and keep you all in His good graces

To the Glory of God Almighty. It is his grace that has brought me to this point in my life. It is my sincere hope those who read this book and espouse a faith in Christ will benefit from my observations and insights. I ask that you judge your beliefs based on Christ's teaching and our Lord's commandments. Beyond that, I can ask no more.

Contents

Acknowledgments

Where I've come from and what I've accomplished over the past several decades in my life in part or in whole are due to the love and support I've received from my best friend, my soul mate, and my wife, Janie. From the outset of our marriage, it's been a team effort. Not so much in the beginning because it took me a while to realize I wasn't single anymore.

Over time, I learned to appreciate her counsel. I learned to look at things from a different perspective that she was able to bring to the table. I thank God for this wonderful, loving, and devoted woman regularly in my prayers. I ask Him to help me to be worthy of her and of the blessing to me that she is. She has been—and continues to be—my rock and my sounding board.

Add this great blessing, along with the blessing of being a born-again Christian, the other blessings in the form of my daughters and grandchildren. No greater blessing has God given me than the love and devotion of family. I will never be able to thank Him enough.

I would also like to acknowledge and thank Eddie Morales for his support and encouragement. While Eddie and I have never met in person, we have in common our love for the martial arts and being cops. Eddie has been the editor/publisher of MartialForce.com. This on-line martial arts magazine has included more than a dozen of my articles, as well as an interview with me regarding my background, rank and experiences in the arts over the past 50 plus years. Eddie has constantly pushed me to write a book. He said he likes the way I write and express myself. Here you go Eddie. And thanks for the support and encouragement you've given me over the past several years.

Lastly my dear friend Rob Debelak, PhD. Rob is an associate professor at Lee University in Cleveland, Tennessee. Our relationship started off in Germany in 1980 when he joined my karate classes. He was eventually promoted to 1st degree black belt and assumed leadership of the classes when I rotated back to the USA in December of 1981. Rob is my senior student, but more importantly he is a dear friend. Over the years as I've written articles I've sent him drafts for review and comment. He has provided me with his counsel and editorial assistance. From time to time I had to remind him he was reviewing and article on such and such subject, not a dissertation. For always being there Rob. Vielen Dank.

Introduction

Over my seventy-plus years of life, I've enjoyed many good times and endured some not-so-good. For the better part of my life, especially the military portion and college years as a student, my political views were fairly "a-political." I never really paid much attention to the partisan bickering and backstabbing that was taking place, whether it was on the local or federal level. Political parties and most of the issues, over which many sparring sessions took place between these people, never resonated with me. When Clinton ran for president, suddenly, politics became important. Many of us on active duty in the military found ourselves asking the question, "How can I respect a president who tells the commandant of the ROTC detachment at his college that he loathes the military?" The answer was simple. I would not be able to respect the man since he clearly didn't respect me or any other military personnel.

Over the past several months, I'd been contemplating writing about my political observations and opinions. This is from the standpoint of a regular small-town guy raised in the Midwest (fly-over country) by a loving pair of Christian parents. The combination of how I was raised; my religious education; my martial arts background; my military career, experiences and travels; my education (bachelor's degree in criminal justice and master's in international relations, with emphasis in counter-terrorism); and my more than four and a half decades as a police officer, coupled with having taught nearly fifteen years as a college political science associate professor, have all impacted my views and opinions.

Because of the nature of how police officers must evaluate things in life, that includes crime and those who commit them, I feel my approach is pragmatic and based on common sense, and the facts. That latter point is the one that frustrates liberals. It seems the facts keep screwing up their agenda to lie to us in an effort to propagandize their socialist goals for our country and our collective way of living.

Let me state for the record: I am not a politician. For the most part, I have little to no respect for the vast majority of them. While I understand the definition incorporates how we interact with others, my reference deals with those who run for some level of public office.

I am a career law enforcement officer, veteran and teacher (both academic subjects and martial arts). I am a husband who is married to his soul mate of more than fifty years. I'm a father of two lovely and talented daughters who have given Janie and me three wonderful grandsons. I am a patriot who willingly served his country in times of war (Vietnam and Desert Storm) and would gladly do so again.

I'm a taxpayer. I'm a person who has worked hard his whole life and is now beginning to enjoy the meager fruits of that labor. I was one of those slow starters in life, but I developed my forward momentum as I got older and more mature. I respect those who have become financially (and otherwise) successful in life. In the majority of these cases, these people have worked hard to get to where they are. They sacrificed and worked long hours. All of that effort has paid off for them. Maybe they invented something that has improved our lives and, in turn, made them wealthy. Regardless of how they've become successful, they're enjoying the fruits of that labor and success.

This stands in contrast to the jealous socialists who envy and covet what these people have attained. These people (liberals) only think about ways of taking it away from the successful. These sorry excuses for humanity can't make it on their own, so they have to hate those who can succeed and have succeeded. This is the politics of envy that democrats use to divide this great country.

Now I do understand many of these liberals are young and have little to no experience in life. They're either working and living at home or attending college, while working, and living at home. The majority of them have no idea what it is to earn a living, pay bills, and plan for the future. Many have no idea what sacrifices are necessary for those who are married and raising a family.

The ones in college are easy prey for the liberal college professors who fill their heads with liberal socialist garbage. They have yet to live, but still they protest and make comments they'll regret when they've grown older, have good jobs and families, and look back through life with more mature and experienced eyes. Mostly because they're driven by their emotions and not common sense based on experience.

But most of all, I'm a Christian American who reveres this country for the freedoms and opportunities it offers—a country with a Constitution and Bill of Rights that protects all citizens.

Now having said up front that I'm a Christian, those who are anti-Christians (people who don't like Christians for some personal reason, maybe because we live with a morale code they reject), agnostics, or atheists will dismiss me as a right-wing zealot and stop at that. In doing so, they demonstrate how myopic they are regarding views that don't fit their agenda or view of their world. They have become the same people who wore brown shirts and attacked those who didn't agree with their dogma in late-1930s Germany. They are the ones who are eroding our First Amendment right to free speech. They prohibit the free exchange of ideas on college campuses from the East to the West Coast. They censure and dictate how we should think and what we can and cannot say. All based on their warped sense of how the world and the USA should be run.

As a person who grew up in small-town America, I was taught that we need to help those unable to help themselves. At the same time, I believe strongly that those who can work as a contributing member of society should do so. If they need training or other educational assistance, we should provide it to them. When that training/ education is over, they need to get to work. Freeloaders are to be discouraged and shunned. People should learn how to be self-sufficient and able to provide for themselves and their loved ones using their God-given talents without asking for handouts. The Bible even tells us this in 2 Thessalonians 3:10: "If a man does not work, neither shall he eat." People are supposed to carry their own weight in life and not burden others unless they've fallen on hard times.

Clearly, there are times when some of us need help. Thankfully, we find that help within our own communities, among charitable neighbors and Christian or other religious institutions. As a child, I remember people stopping by our home who were not known to me. I would ask my mom who they were. She would tell me they were homeless people in need of help. She always provided them with food and used clothing, based on their needs. Mom and Dad both told us kids that Christians seek to help those in need. As a family, we were blessed and able to provide charitable assistance to these folks. This is a practice my family and I still engage in today.

I'm also someone who has learned the importance of a strong personal and national defense. That means I clearly understand it is the strong who will survive. The weak, who hide behind others, will ultimately perish when and where anarchy is allowed to take root. Because of this, I've developed my skill sets for self-defense, both with and without a weapon. I've learned how to treat emergency medical situations. I've learned how to survive in the outdoors. I've also learned how to detect liars and scam artists who would try to cheat my family and me out of what we've worked a lifetime creating.

I fully believe those of us in the military and law enforcement are the sheepdogs responsible for protecting the sheep (average citizens) of our society from the wolves and sociopaths who seek to victimize and consume them. People who put their faith in the police showing up to save them are delusional. When things happen, seconds count. A normal police response varies from seven to twenty-five minutes (depending on whether you live in the city or out in the county). When your survival or that of your loved ones is at stake, those few minutes are a lifetime. You either prepare for your own defense and survival or perish.

To be self-sufficient and focused on one's own preservation must be the word of the day. No, I'm not a doomsayer or survivalist living in a cave. I'm a realist who has lived and traveled in enough places on this planet to know the dangers that exist and the evil that waits for the gullible and stupid among us.

I clearly understand it is through God's grace that we go through this life. When He chooses to call us home, we must be ready in our hearts. Here lies one of the great differences between people of faith and those without it. As Christians, we have hope. We have the knowledge we will one day be in heaven with our Lord and Savior Jesus Christ. Nonbelievers don't have any such hope. All they have is that one day, they will die and everything ends. What a truly sad way to live out one's short time on this earth.

Because of the lessons of the two World Wars, Korea, Vietnam, and subsequent Cold War, I've learned about the dangers presented by too much Socialism (a case on point is Venezuela today), or any form of Communism. In order for free people to remain so, those they elect to office should be stalwart supporters of our country's founding documents. When politicians begin telling us those documents are archaic and out of date with the times (as is the case with several Democrats like O'Rourke, Feinstein, Pelosi, Harris, Ocasio-Cortez, Warren, and others), we should shun them like the plague, for they are utterly anathema to continued freedom, prosperity, and survival of America.

Such is the case with the current crop of candidates who are Democratic presidential hopefuls. We're a few months away from the 2020 presidential elections and already some twenty liberal Democrats have announced their candidacy. From Warren, who has shown herself to be a fraud willing to claim Indian status in order gain votes and extra consideration as a student and when seeking jobs, now promising to pay off everyone's student loans, to O'Rourke, who wants to tear down all the Southern Border fencing and walls in order to create open borders, to Bernie Sanders, who wants to give convicted felons the right to vote. Each of them seems willing to "out liberal" the other. The more they talk and promise, the more intelligent people see them for the phonies they truly are. The promises and pie-in-the-sky dreams they're pushing will never come to pass. Their only explanation for how they plan to pay for everything is by taking more money from hard working Americans by raising taxes.

They continue to fail. With some one hundred and fifty or so years of examples to learn from they still fail to recognize that socialism only brings misery and poverty to those less fortune who liberals have convinced they're trying to help. One need only examine cities like Detroit and Flint in Michigan, Chicago and St. Louis in Illinois, Baltimore Maryland, Oakland and San Francisco in California to name but a few. Where the people have elected democrats to rule their respective cities crime and poverty have resulted. Sadly, the uniformed masses who make up a large segment of our American society will not know or understand this until it's too late. Even then some of these people will never have that epiphany where the light of reality comes on.

People who sincerely believe and follow the teachings of Karl Marx are devoid of reality and ignore the lessons of history that have shown communism to be an utter failure. No place or time in history has Marx's ideological views of a utopian society ever come to pass. In each and every case, Communism has resulted in a small number of the strong controlling the larger group of the weak and ignorant through the use of the military. There is and never has been a society that was completely equal in all aspects (a utopia). Here again the sad fact is this is exactly what leftist politicians want us to believe. Uneducated masses who willingly suck up the lies, as long as they get free stuff in turn—or at least the promise of it.

One key and important example of an early attempt at socialism was the Plymouth Rock experiment of 1620. In this situation, those pilgrims had entered into a contract whereby all fruits of labor were placed into a central pool where citizens would draw an equal share (a commune). It failed then, as it has to this date, because there will always be those people who will not do their share and contribute but will willingly take from others who've done the work. These are people who are lazy and only want to get by on handouts paid for by others.

That is something the late President Lyndon Johnson and his liberal ilk of the middle 1960s didn't understand when they created welfare (his Great Society plan), thinking that would be the panacea to eradicate poverty. It has been nothing but a complete failure. Today, there is greater poverty than what existed in Johnson's day. There are tens of thousands who receive welfare subsidized by our tax dollars pushed by liberal socialist Democrats. They were naïve in Johnson's day as they are today some fifty-plus years later.

Yet to this day, there are those who are so arrogant as to believe they can make this dream of a socialistic society (communism) happen because they are smarter than the people who have tried it before them. These are the academic intellectuals who live in books and have literally no clue about the rest of the world and the poverty and strife that exist there. They are devoid of reality as are so many on the left of our country who've been educated by these same academics who no longer teach the true history of our country and the importance of it. These are people whose only knowledge of the world is based on biased news feeds and Hollywood movies and TV sitcoms. Were they to live in other counties and travel outside their small communities, they would have their eyes opened.

I've also come to see the majority of politicians today as liars, backstabbers, and power-hungry profiteers. They are the dregs of our society whose only goal is money and power. They declare themselves servants of the people concerned only with the well-being of America. Nothing could be farther from the truth. They are the carnival barkers who sell their snake oil to any fool willing to listen.

They will readily destroy anyone who stands in their way by any means available. The people who support and vote for them have fallen for the lies and false promises for so long they are no longer able to see or understand the truth. Like the weak-minded people who followed Jim Jones and David Koresh, they are unable to apply common sense to issues and situations that regularly plague our country. They fall for the pie-in-the-sky proposals made by these "pide piper" politicians. They are the Kool-Aid drinkers of America who are incapable of applying logic to their assessments of current situations.

The left's willingness to destroy those they don't like or with whom they disagree was present for all to see when Trump was sworn in as our president. The visceral hatred and loathing these people have for him are pathological, almost to the point of bordering on sociopathic, in their feelings, attitudes, and behaviors.

It was also clearly apparent in the attacks by Feinstein and other deceitful leftist politicians on Justice Brett Kavanaugh. He was falsely accused by Christine Blasey Ford of having sexually assaulted her. What's so amazing about this are her claims. While she accused him of sexual abuse, she couldn't tell anyone where it happened. She also was unable to give any specifics or evidence—whatsoever. Then as if this wasn't bad enough for her credibility, four of the people she claimed were there said they weren't. She may have been assaulted at some time and place in her past. If so, why can't she remember? I remember tragic events in my life like they were yesterday.

What's interesting to note in the case involving Ford and Kavanaugh was the timing of the accusation. Ford had communicated with Feinstein in July of that year (2016) about the alleged sexual assault upon her person by Brett Kavanaugh. Ford asked Feinstein to keep things confidential. Once Kavanaugh was nominated by President Trump, the Ford accusations began appearing in the media. Feinstein said neither she nor her staff leaked the information about the assault claims to the media. Because of the nature of liberals, and observations of their past conduct, I do not believe Feinstein. She, like others in her party and on the left, especially in the media, have shown a strong propensity to say whatever is needed at the time. The truth has little to do with it. It's all about the spin and their agenda. A bit of old wisdom tells us if you tell a lie often and long enough, it eventually becomes true in the majority of people's minds.

One must ask a simple question though. Why did this claim by Ford not come out until September–October timeframe, just as Kavanaugh was nominated to the Supreme Court, when it was made known to Feinstein nearly three months before? From my perspective, it was a timing issue. Had it come out too early, it would not have had the effect or impact it did after Kavanaugh's nomination. It's clearly all part and parcel of the political game of cutthroat politicians' play in order to destroy their opposition. The Democrats tried their best, but in the end, they failed.

The presumption of innocence or the appropriate applications of due process were totally ignored and trampled into the dirt by Democrats as they moved forward in a blind rage to pillory and convict Mr. Kavanaugh, merely because he was Trump's nominee for the Supreme Court. This is a prime example of the lengths and depths liberal Democrats and their supporters will go. For me, there is no question this country needs term limits—badly. I'll address how that can take place toward the end of the book.

Add to this miserable mix their willing accomplices and eager lapdogs in the media, and I truly fear for the future of our country. I'm talking about the three networks—ABC, CBS, and NBC. There is also the cable crowd made up of channels like MSNBC, CNBC, CNN, and PBS. These are people who call themselves journalists. What far too many of them are, are die-hard propagandist and liars. They either take and spin the truth to meet their needs, or they out-right manufacture and lie about the facts.

A recent case in point was the BuzzFeed report by Jacobs who told everyone Trump's personal lawyer Cohen had admitted that Trump had told him to lie to Congress regarding real estate deals in Russia. The mainstream media ran rampant with the story all day, salivating like Pavlovian dogs at the prospect of Trump being impeached. These are people who use Russian-style disinformation and function like the Soviet's state-run media. You can also liken them to Hitler supporters who used Nazi-style Goebbels propaganda tactics to shore up their liberal friends in politics while doing every-thing in their power to destroy the opposition. The BuzzFeed report turned out to be a complete lie.

Another example of the media's rush to judge is how they han-dled what transpired during a "Right to Life" march. A group of high school students from Covington Catholic High School, Kentucky, were in Washington DC by the Lincoln Memorial on January 18 of this year (2019) participating in the march when a man in Indian dress (later identified as Nathan Phillips), beating an Indian-style drum and performing Indian chants, purposely approached one of the students. The high school junior, Nicholas Sandmann, didn't move as Phillips intentionally approached him while he continued beating his drum and chanting. Phillips stopped a very short distance from Sandmann and continued chanting and beating his drum in Nick Sandmann's face.

All the while this is taking, place a group of black Hebrew Israelites (as they refer to themselves) can be heard yelling crass, vile, and extremely vulgar things about the boys and Trump from a distance. Little was made of this in the media. One has to wonder if the reason for that is that these antagonists were black. This has become the mannerisms displayed by liberal leftists in today's society. If these people represent a religion, how can they be as confrontational and negative using the language they used? It flies in the face of what true religions stand for.

The media immediately accused Nick of being rude and disrespectful and of having started the whole thing. A key reason for this rush to punish by the media was the fact Nick was wearing a Trump Make America Great Again (MAGA) hat. This rush to judge and persecution reporting by the mainstream media resulted in numerous threats of violence and death against the boys and their school over social media and phone calls.

With the passage of time, others began reviewing all the videos available. This resulted in full disclosure of the whole story. The students were found to have not conducted themselves inappropriately, as reported. They were completely exonerated. Further investigation found Phillips to be an activist who purposely instigated the confrontation.

A few weeks later, lawyers representing the Covington High School students filed a $250 million lawsuit against the *Washington Post*, who was aware of the complete contents of the videos but chose to slander and malign the students anyway. A second and third lawsuit for $275 million have since been brought against CNN and MSNBC. The lawyers for these teenagers have stated other lawsuits will be forthcoming.

Just the other day, as the government was preparing the paperwork that will go out for next year's census, the court ruled the Trump administration could not include a question about citizenship. Immediately the press started telling everyone the Trump administration had back down and was no longer interested in adding the citizenship question. Later that day Trump sent out a tweet denying this and telling everyone he still planned on having that question added. This was the latest in a long line of examples of how the people in the press, both print and on TV, lie and distort the truth when it comes to Trump.

Trump has aptly named the mainstream media as the purveyors of "fake news" since he was sworn into the office of the president. The media's conduct and constant reporting of lies and accusation, only to have them refuted, has clearly earned them the title President Trump has labeled them with. Knowing that at least 85 percent of people in the media are registered Democrats speaks volumes as well. Whatever happened to honest, objective reporting?

The media reports on negative stories involving Republicans and Conservatives with enthusiastic glee while ignoring those involving Democrats and the left. When a negative story involves the left, the media will place emphasis on how those on the right reacted toward the screw-ups on the left, making it appear that Conservatives are mean-spirited and disrespectful toward them. The media's efforts are to always display those on the right (Republicans and Conservative supporters) in as negative a way as possible. They will hardly ever portray conservatives in a positive light, unless there's no way around it other than not reporting it at all.

With the exception of those in the loony tunes left who drink up every lie by these media propagandists (because it feeds their agenda), the vast majority of Americans see today's journalists for what and who they really are. We are blessed in this country to have other outlets like Fox News and Fox Nation on cable and the Internet, or radio personalities like Rush Limbaugh, Sean Hannity, Laura Ingram, and Dana Loesch, to name but a few who provide candid and honest reporting of the facts. These folks truly shine the light of truth in the dark corners or our society where the rats and cockroaches try to hide.

Sadly, those who only speak Spanish and listen to Univision, Telemundo, and other such outlets only hear the same lies that English listeners hear from the aforementioned leftist networks and channels. There are no alternative Spanish networks or talk shows to counter these leftist liars and propagandists on the Spanish channels.

I know some will not like what I have to say here and in the following pages. Others will agree to some extent, some without any reservations. Such is the nature of what makes us human beings. I respect your right to disagree, just as I expect you to respect my right to do the same.

I do not respect people who are so closed-minded (ideologues) that they will not entertain for a second that someone else might have a valid point or argument. These are the haters on the left (and the far right) who clearly have clinical and psychological problems. They attack or confront people they disagree with in public places, showing no respect for the person they're abusing verbally, or the friends or family members with them. They do so in mass because that is the nature of cowards. Case in point are those who identify themselves as/or with antifa (standing for antifascist). They dress in black, hide their faces, and attack like a pack of dogs those they disagree with. The irony is they are conducting themselves as anarchist, which flies in the face of what they call themselves. Singularly, they are gutless.

The first part of my book will deal with how and where I was raised. It will follow my growing up, my education, my years of training and studies in the martial arts, my military years and law enforcement careers, as well as other life experiences. The purpose for this preamble (as it were) is to set the stage for why my political views and opinions have evolved to the point they're at today.

Throughout my upbringing, Christian principles and teachings have always been present. Since Supreme Court decisions in the 1962 and '63 time frames removed our ability to pray in school, read the Bible, or even post the Ten Commandments, the moral compass of our country has been badly off course. Sadly, this new direction has taken us, as a people and country, farther away from our Heavenly Father and the teachings of peace, love, hope, and charity as illustrated to us in both the Old and New Testaments.

The Ten Commandments teach us not to lie, covet what others have, bear false witness against others, and so on. All these are aspects that are readily apparent and visible in the daily attitudes and conduct of those on the left, and to some extent of those on the right as well.

My goal in this book is to put before the reader a simple question. How do your religious beliefs stack up against/with those politicians you vote for and support? If the politicians and party you support conduct themselves contrary to the biblical teachings you were raised with and have studied, why do you continue to support them? In doing so you are complicit in their sinfulness. You are a co-conspirator because you suborn the sinful nature of these people and what they stand for. How can you ask God for forgiveness while supporting these people? This is something only you can answer. It's between you and God. You must give this serious thought and reflection.

For those who are a part of the big-city liberal mind-set, I'm that gun-toting, gospel-singing, NRA-supporting (life member, Patriot Patron, and Golden Eagle), pickup-driving, small-town American patriot who still believes there is greatness in this country and that God our Father has blessed it since the day the USA was founded.

I don't give a damn for those who threaten and bully others, whether on some social media platform or in person backed by a mob. Facebook, Twitter, and other social media platforms allow these cowards a place to hide. It allows them to feel they have power over others.

The reality is they are people who have miserable lives and can't stand to see anyone else enjoying life, being successful, or just plain being happy. In a word, they're losers. While I'm willing to turn the other cheek in many situations, there are other times and situations where I will readily stand up against evil and defend myself and those unable to defend themselves.

Christians who understand God's love and the many blessings He showers us with are happy and content with what he has given us. We understand God gives us that with which He feels we are capable of using properly and generously.

Clearly, there are those who suffer in great poverty around the world. Christians of various denominations/organizations make every effort to provide food, medicine, education, and other types of assistance as best they can, all based on the generosity of those of their faith. They understand God provides for us, each unto his needs. Now the journey begins.

Growing Up Hoosier

My Parents

I was born on October 4, 1947. My natural mother was a fourteen-year-old teenager from Peru, Indiana. At the time of my birth, she was staying at the Suemma Coleman Home for Women on North Illinois Street in Indianapolis, Indiana. This was a special home for unwed mothers (teenagers). Young girls could stay at the home until they delivered their child. Once the delivery was complete, the child was put up for adoption. I know virtually nothing about her save what my (adopted) mother told me.

At two months of age, I was adopted by Doctor and Mrs. Adron A. Sullenger. Dad was a radiologist and mom was a registered nurse (BSN). They were in their early thirties and adopted because my father was epileptic and didn't want to pass the disease along to any children. I don't know if that would have happened, but he was not going to take any chances. Later, a younger brother (Steven Ray) was adopted followed by, a few years after that, our younger sister Sue Ellen. Each of us was brought into the family at around two months of age.

My mother when she graduated from nursing school from Indiana University's School of Nursing

Understanding what it means to be adopted has a different meaning for each individual. For me, it was God placing me in a better home with a loving couple who wanted children, whether their own or from someone else. These people are the only parents I've ever known. They raised me and my siblings as Christians. For that, I am eternally grateful.

Now having said that, I must also confess I didn't see that quite so clearly in my younger years. I recall on a few occasions when I was embroiled in one of my tantrums or upset about something or other, I would tell my mother that she didn't love me. I would say no one loved me. Otherwise, why was I given away? Why didn't my real mother want me? Of course at that age, I had no idea. I was too young and immature to understand the trail of life and why a young girl might be placed in a situation where it was necessary to give up a child.

Good, loving parents don't have to be blood related. The love, devotion, and nurturing we received from them, coupled with their teaching us how to be productive Christian members of our American society, have resulted in my appreciation for all they did and for God's greatness in placing me in their home and guiding me through life to this day. As the cliché goes, hindsight is 20/20.

(front row left to right) My sister Sue Ellen,
my brother Steve and me. In the back row (left to
right) are my sister June, mom, dad and Alberta

23

Mom and Dad also brought in two sisters, Alberta and June Brock, who became big sisters to my brother, sister, and I. They were already starting high school. June, the younger of the two, was about seven years older than me. Alberta was nine years older. Once Alberta and June graduated from high school, Dad asked them what post-high school education they'd like to choose. Alberta chose a nursing school while June chose to go to a beauty college where she learned how to cut hair and do all the latest hairstyling fashions women enjoyed.

When my father was in his senior year of medical school, working toward becoming a surgeon, he became an epileptic. He suffered grand mal seizures. These seizures would cause him to pass out, remaining unconscious for several minutes. Mom would instruct us kids to stay clear in order to give Dad time to come back to his senses. It was scary at first, but later, we became more knowledgeable and understanding. Because of the disease, Dad changed his focus from surgery to radiology. This meant he would have less doctor-patient interface. His focus was always on others.

My dad at his graduation from Medical School
from Indiana University's School of Medicine

My mother was a stay-home mom who raised us kids with the help of a lady named Mary Smith. Because Mary was black and like a second mother to us, I had difficulty in understanding why some whites felt the way they did about black people in our city. As I grew older, I began seeing this on a larger scale. Mary helped our mother raise us kids and watched over us when Mom had to drive Dad to his various work locations. Mom was quiet and easygoing. She made sure we had clean clothes, hot food, and clean home and environment to grow up in. Her love and concern for us kids were always apparent. Between Mom and Mary, we were taught the differences between right and wrong. We were praised when we were good and punished when we weren't.

Dad had grown up without a father from the age of fourteen, much as I had. He was born in Sebree, Kentucky, and moved with his family later to Boonville, Indiana. It was while they lived in Boonville that my grandfather Sullenger died. I don't recall if it was from a stroke or heart attack. Dad was an Eagle Scout and member of the Order of the Arrow. Dad was very self-sufficient, determined, and a quick learner. He invented something to do with preparing blood by separating the plasma from the red and white cells while he was working at Eli Lilly. I'm not really clear on what it all entailed. What I do know is it paid for his college and medical school.

Dad was also a strict disciplinarian. He didn't believe in the concept of "spare the rod and spoil the child." If we got into trouble, we were punished in a manner that fit the crime. All too often that meant a spanking. For those of you country folk reading this, that would be an ass-whooping. If we were at Grandma Cottingham's farmhouse in rural Central Indiana, it meant being instructed to cut a branch off the willow tree in the backyard. Ouch! Either way you refer to it, we got the message when it took place. There was nothing missing in the translation.

We also knew we were punished out of love. If that's not clear, that tells me a lot about how you were raised. If you didn't heed his admonishments when you did something wrong, he would emphasize the point with the paddle. As I look back over those years, I appreciate what he, my mother, Mary, and my Grandma Cottingham all did. I understand they did it because they loved us and wanted us, kids, to have a clear understanding between what was right and what was wrong. They wanted us to grow up as responsible adults.

Our father was also a person who valued honesty and integrity. He told us kids if we did something wrong and didn't tell him, the punishment would be harsh. On the other hand, if we told him what we did and were honest, while we would still get punished, it wouldn't be as severe. He took us at our word if he asked us about something. If he found out we had lied, we'd be punished for it. He wanted to ensure we clearly understood the value we should place on our word when it was given. Unlike politicians today who say they'll do something or that they stand for something, only to change direction when talking with a group or person who didn't see things that way. These people will do or say anything for a vote.

Our father also taught us the important lessons of kindness and generosity based on biblical teachings. Dad's heart was really big. While a person who believed deeply in honor and integrity, he also believed in the importance of the Christian charity and helping others. I saw this firsthand when he hired Regis Mart Theriac (born November 13, 1918, in Vincennes, Indiana) to be his driver. After becoming an epileptic, Dad wouldn't drive. He had an earlier man who drove for him when I was younger. I can't even remember what he looked like let alone his name. When the need arose, Mom would drive Dad to his various work destinations.

Reg, as everyone called him, was a survivor of the Bataan Death March that took place during World War II in the Pacific. The day after Japan attacked the US Naval and Air installations at Pearl Harbor on the Hawaiian Islands, they also began their attack on the Philippines. On April 9, 1942, approximately seventy-five thousand US and Philippine troops were captured and forced to endure a sixty-five-mile forced march under extremely harsh conditions and treatment by the Japanese soldiers. Thousands died as a result of injury, disease, malnutrition, or at the hands of a Japanese soldier who would execute them if they couldn't keep up. Reg had difficulty holding down a job because he suffered from periodic bouts of malaria and other ailments, all the result of his captivity and treatment by the Japanese. When my father hired Reg, he told him whenever he was sick and unable to come into work, he was to stay home and call. Dad said, "Cuma can drive me where I need to go."

Cuma was Mom's name. She was born Cuma Fern Cottingham and met Dad while working as a nurse in Indianapolis, Indiana. She and Dad were both products of the Indiana University Medical School. Mom was a farm girl raised by Cash and Bessie Cottingham on a rural country farm just east of Kokomo, Indiana, just outside the small town of Nevada. I have many fond memories of farm life from the frequent visits with our grandparents. As grandpa Cash got older he ran a small store in Neveda, Indiana, and was also appointed the Post Master General of Sharpsville, Indiana. I still have the certificate signed by Franklin D. Roosevelt in March of 1936 hanging on my wall.

My mother's parents, Cash and Bessie Cottingham

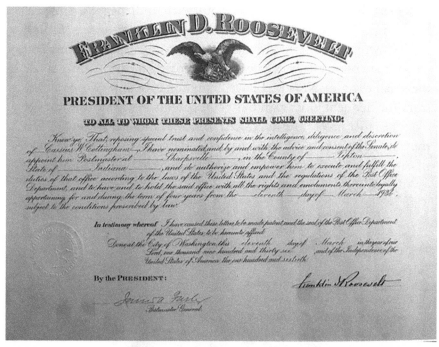

Certificate of Appointment to Post Master General
of the City of Sharpsville, Indiana. Singed by
Franklin D. Roosevelt, March 11, 1939

During the summertime, we kids would spend a week or two with them learning the chores that came with that lifestyle. We learned to ride horses, get eggs from the large chicken coop, feed the pigs, shovel manure from the barns (later to be spread around the fields), and to drive the tractors. We learned what it took to kill and prepare a chicken for dinner. We learned about the realities of life and what it takes for people to survive.

As a radiologist, my father had his own office where local doctors could send patients for various types of x-rays and other radiological services. He also provided these services to various hospitals within a forty-mile radius. Those small cities with hospitals but no radiologist on staff would hire Dr. A. A. Sullenger as their part-time radiologist. Dad would travel to places like Lawrenceville, Olney, and Robertson, all across the Wabash River in Illinois. He also helped the Good Samaritan Hospital in Vincennes and drove regularly to Jasper, Indiana, to read film and provide a diagnosis to the Catholic hospital there.

Whenever Dad was in Olney working for their hospital, he would get his Ford worked on at the local Ford dealership. He had a favorite mechanic there who had been trying to get a loan to open his own shop. I remember he was a nice man as well as a hard worker. The banks wouldn't make the loan to him, so my father did. Sadly, I can't recall the man's name. Dad helped him relocate to Vincennes, where he established his new auto mechanic's shop.

Other examples of Dad's generosity were him providing financial assistance by paying for Mary Smith's daughter and our neighbor's (Mr. Abraham) daughter to attend nursing school. Dad also orchestrated the complete repainting of Mr. Abraham's home since he was elderly and unable to afford the work let alone accomplish it himself.

After organizing and planning with other neighbors, a weekend was set aside and the painting of the home accomplished. I still recall my Mom walking around with a large plate of sandwiches and a pitcher of lemonade. It was a wonderful example of neighbors coming together in the spirit of Christian charity to help someone in need.

My mom standing with a can of paint by Mr. Arbams house
the weekend dad and the neighborhood painted his house

My dad squatting by the porch painting the railing. Mr. Abrams
can be seen standing on the left of the picture facing the camera

It was lessons like these that instilled in me and my siblings the importance of helping those who, for whatever reason, cannot help themselves. This is just another example of the one I mentioned in the introduction regarding those homeless people who stopped by the house for a meal and whatever else we were able to provide them.

Dad was also an accomplished carpenter and woodworker. He had a workshop in our basement that would have been the envy of anybody who loved working with wood. He built a playhouse for our sister Sue Ellen. He'd built a functional grandfather clock that used wooden works and counterweights. Later, when some of the wooden parts began to break or fail, he replaced them with mechanical ones. The face, hands, and number of the clock were also all made out of handcrafted wood. The workmanship was as good as any master carpenter could hope to create. Oh, and that's one of the key reasons Steve and I never tried to make his paddle disappear. It was futile.

My father also taught us kids the importance of working hard and saving. We each got an allowance. In order to earn that allowance, we had our respective chores to do. Each of us had to keep our rooms clean and our beds made every morning. Other chores included helping Mom by washing the dishes, mowing the lawn (with a push mower no less—thank God for a small yard), raking the leaves, shoveling the snow off the drive and sidewalk, keeping the trash containers empty, and so on.

As I got old enough to begin playing baseball, I needed to buy a glove. Dad took me down to Van Meters Sporting Goods on the Main Street of downtown Vincennes. We picked out a nice glove, and I ponied up what cash I'd saved. Since I was lacking nearly $15, Dad kicked in the rest. Over the next several months, I paid him back out of the allowance I earned.

That same scenario also took place after my younger brother, Steve, caused me to break a basement window. He was in his normal mode of harassing and irritating me. As a result, I attempted to hit him by throwing a stick. He dodged it, and the stick broke the window. When Dad came home from work, I decided to tell him about what had taken place. He'd always told us kids to be honest if we did something wrong. This was my chance to put that to the test. I recounted the events as they had happened and waited. After a short moment of silence, he said he was proud of me for being honest. He said because of that, there would be no spanking (to my great relief). He said I would have to pay for the repair and replacement of the window from my allowance. I would also be grounded for a week.

There were other similar lessons regarding being responsible. In short, Dad wanted us kids to be honest and honorable in our daily lives. He wanted us to live as Christians and treat people with brotherly love according to Christ's teachings. Because of the way he treated everyone he came in contact with, the church was overflowing on the day of his funeral. This included several nuns who had traveled from the Catholic Hospital in Jasper to show their respects as well as attending our Protestant service.

My Religious Upbringing and Elementary School

I started as many kids do with Mom and Dad taking us to church on Sunday mornings. This included Sunday school when we were a little older followed by the main service. Dad and Mom were members at the Presbyterian Church in Vincennes that was across the street from the main post office (today, it's where the city's police department is located). As kids, my brother and I were nonstop on the move during the services. Mom would make some comment to Dad about the boys having ants in their pants. A sharp word or look from Dad normally had the necessary chilling effect and resulted in a short period of quiet. This was the denomination in which I was baptized.

After finding out that I was not passing my first-grade class in the public elementary school because I needed glasses, I started the first grade over again the following year at St. John's Lutheran School. They didn't have me repeat the class at the public school because the teacher had me sitting in the rear of the class and had made no effort to ascertain why I wasn't doing well. Mom and Dad were not happy about this lack of concern on her part.

I completed all eight grades of my elementary and middle school years at St John's Lutheran before starting my freshman year at Lincoln High School. The religious education continued also at the Presbyterian Church and St. John's during daily catechism classes, culminating in my confirmation in both faiths.

Throughout my growing-up years, we studied the Bible and tried to practice Christ's teachings. Because of my sinful nature, this

MICHAEL A. SULLENGER

was all but impossible. Steve Green's song "I Repent" said it best. "Though your love is in me, it doesn't always win me when competing with my sin." After hearing that song for the first time, it was like I'd taken a deep chest wound from a spear. It was songs like that one and others that ministered to my heart.

One of my many blessings has been a good voice. I did help it along somewhat during my undergraduate years by taking four semesters of applied voice with the director of the vocal department at UT Pan American. Without a doubt, the music ministry is powerful beyond belief. After graduating from Pan Am and returning to the Air Force, I continued singing at religious services, both Protestant and Catholic, until my retirement.

Later in life, after Janie and I had retired from the Air Force, I would sing with the song leaders' group as well as performing special music (solos) at St. Paul's Lutheran Church and School in McAllen, Texas. I would ask God to bless me and the music. I would ask Him to use me as the instrument through which the Holy Spirit could touch the hearts of those present and that He would allow the music to minister to the spiritual needs of those present as it had for me. I can't tell you how many times I saw the emotional effects of my music when I sang. It was clearly evident in the teary eyes of countless petitioners who were in the audience that the Holy Spirit was present and ministering to their hearts and needs.

Over the years, I visited a couple of other churches, offering to provide my gift of musical ministry to their congregations. One location was in Edinburg on McColl Street just south of Freddy Gonzalez. The other church was on Loop 499 in Harlingen (where we moved after I started teaching at Texas State Technical College), across from a newly constructed elementary school.

The first church allowed me to sing during one of their services. When I tried to get acquainted with some of the musicians in that church all I got was a cold shoulder. The second location didn't even give me the courtesy of a reply or acknowledgment. I've often wondered why they have this attitude when they are supposed to represent the love and kindness our Savior teaches us in the New Testament.

34

Over the years I've come to understand just because a church represents the House of God, it's the people inside who either make it truly a place for Christians to unite in leaning and praise, or it's a place for narcissistic egos to be on display. The church family are a reflection of its leader/pastor.

The Pain of Losing
a Loved One

During the summer of '62, we lost my dad. It was July 8, a Sunday. It was the summer before I started high school. I was fourteen years old, just like my father was when he lost his dad. I was off with a girl I liked (Linda Hanson) and her church group, another Lutheran Church in town, at Spring Mill State Park. The park is located in Mitchell, Indiana, and to this day has a fully functional pioneer village. When the bus got back to the church in Vincennes, I was surprised to find the pastor from our Presbyterian church waiting for me instead of my mother.

As we drove back to Lake Lawrence where our lakefront cottage was located, across the Wabash River in Illinois, Pastor Knock told me my dad had drowned. Even today, more than fifty-six years later, it seems like only yesterday. The emptiness, the feelings of pain and sadness at his loss are still fresh. I found out Dad had gone swimming in the lake before lunch and had a seizure. Dr. Ralph Smith, our next-door neighbor at the lake, attempted to save my father. It wasn't possible because of the length of time he'd been underwater. Dr. Smith had his offices in the same building as my dad's and worked closely with him over the years.

Mom was a wreck. Not just because of the loss of the man she loved deeply but also because they'd had an argument before he'd gone for the swim. Mom didn't want him swimming alone as she feared he'd have a seizure. She lived with the regret of not having told him she loved him one last time until her death in January of 1983.

I'd never really experience the loss of a loved one who was really close to me until that day. We had lost my Grandpa Cash (my mother's father) a year or so earlier to cancer, but we only saw them a few times a year. The pain of losing my father was terrible. Add to this the fact Dad and I had not been on best of terms because I had become more confrontational and rebellious. The sense of emptiness along with the resounding question of "WHY?" seemed to swim around my head. It wasn't until my older sister Alberta asked me, "Why would God do this?" that my question was answered.

In responding to her, I found myself answering my own question regarding why. Here is where one's faith manifests itself when one is hurting and in need. I told Alberta I really didn't know why God had taken Dad. I just felt He had a reason. I told her we may never know why, but we had to have faith in the fact that our Heavenly Father had a good reason. We needed to be strong in order to help Mom with the chores and duties she was left with. We needed to be there for her as she dealt with the loss of our father. We needed to do our best to live the way we knew Dad expected us to. That was as Christians.

Sadly, that was an area I still managed to mess up. Throughout high school, my growing rebellious nature caused my mom and grandma (her mom) constant problems. I know I was a disappointment to them both during that time of my life. A combination of bad grades and confrontations with the police, along with a bad attitude and rebelliousness, made for several years of bad times and hurt feelings. Thankfully, those years were locked away, and I was able to continue on in my life. As mentioned earlier, I was a slow starter. Eventually, I managed to begin moving forward and learning positive ways to participate in my family and my community.

Since our marriage, I've encouraged and supported my wife with her parents. I've told her she must take advantage of spending time with them, to assist and care for them whenever and wherever possible. People who are able to enjoy their parents into their eighties and nineties are blessed. Those of us who lost are parents at a younger age eventually come to understand this.

After retiring in June of 1993, we had returned to Texas. Janie had noted during her parents' visit with us in Illinois the realization that they were growing older. We lost her dad in August of 2000. He would have turned eighty that October. Her mother is now ninety-three and living in a nursing home. Several years ago, she began developing dementia and required someone with her 24/7. This resulted in Janie retiring at age sixty-two so she could be there for her mom.

Around this same time, her mother's dementia was causing her to become aggressive and go after her cousin Jose Fina. Fina, now eighty-five, was moved in with us as it was apparent she would be better off. Since Fina suffers with asthma, diabetes, hypertension, and arthritis, to name a few ailments, we were in a better position to ensure she received medical care and made her doctor's appointments as the need demanded.

Living in other countries and learning about other cultures has resulted in an awareness of how Americans treat their elderly, as compared with other cultures. Oriental cultures revere and care for their elderly until they pass on. Americans warehouse them in assisted-living facilities in order to not have to deal with them. Why is it we fail to recognize and respect the wealth of knowledge and wisdom our senior citizens have? Having said this, I realize some folks are not financially or emotionally able to support or provide for their elderly parents. We each must endeavor to do our best in this area. One day, we'll be the elder family members relying on our children and their largess and compassion.

High School

When I started high school that fall of 1962, I didn't really know anyone except those who had graduated with me from St. John's. I found a number of the students were familiar with me and our family's loss. They made it a point of sharing their condolences and understanding of it. They also made an effort to make me feel welcome.

As mentioned a few paragraphs back that my grades in high school weren't great. Actually, that can also be said for my earlier years at St John's. I really had not put forth much effort with my studies. Probably because I had trouble staying focused and trying to read about subjects that were less than interesting. I also found I had difficulties in comprehending math, beyond the basics.

Mom and Dad had hired our postman Mr. Levenhagen, who was also a member of St. John's Lutheran Church and a regular soloist, to tutor my brother, Steve, and me. Needless to say, he had his hands full with two boys who were nonstop on the move. I have no doubt in today's environment, we'd both have been diagnosed as having ADHD or ADD. It wasn't until I'd finished four years in the United States Air Force and was married that I began to apply myself during my years at Pan American University, realizing more of my potential (more on that a little later).

During my freshman year at Lincoln High, I attempted to play football, only to pull a groin muscle. During my seventh and eighth grade years at St. John's, I'd played on the basketball team. At five feet ten inches in height, I wasn't able to fight for the ball under the boards when taller players could out jump me while playing in the middle school grades. It didn't take long before I realized trying to compete at the high school level with even bigger students in both football and basketball was not going to go very far either.

I participated in the high school band during my freshman and half of my sophomore years before dropping out. I played the cornet during my freshman year but was made to learn the tuba, baritone, and bass drum during my sophomore year by the new bandleader, Walter Boyd. Boyd had replaced Mr. Hal Meurer, who was better liked by most of the members of the band. While I had one of the best sounds on the cornet and the highest range of any of the others, I couldn't sight-read music well. The new guy and I didn't hit it off.

I was more interested in extracurricular activities as a teenage boy. This included the normal young man's interest in young ladies and going out on the occasional date. But my primary interest, and subsequent love, was training and studying the martial arts.

I was also part of a rock-and-roll band called the Misfits during my high school years. After Dad died, Mom bought me a Rickenbacker single pickup guitar, along with a Fender Tremolux piggyback amplifier. As I learned to play, I began to get together with some of my classmates who also played different instruments (drums, lead guitar, bass, and keyboard). I played rhythm guitar and sang backup. We traveled around, playing at different high school dances within a fifty-mile range, at the occasional bar, or at the teen center in Vincennes; lots of great memories from those days.

Because I was not part of the "jock" or "in group" in my class, I began being ridiculed by some of the others in the so-called in crowd. The one who seemed to always be leading the charge was a guy named Tom Kizer. Kizer seemed to take joy in poking fun at people he didn't appear to care much for. Because I worked out with weights and was developing a better build than most (and he was on the fat and pudgy side), he tagged me with the nickname *Tarzan*. That name later was reversed to *Nazart* and then shortened to *Naz*. Kizer liked to be the center of attention as much as possible. In reality, he was tolerated by many and disliked by most (even though that was never shared with him) because of his obnoxious and irritating attitude and mannerisms. Dealing with his bully-like tactics became the norm.

40

Later at the twenty-fifth high school reunion, I had the opportunity to reconnect with many of my classmates. Kizer was there and just as mouthy and obnoxious as always. I remember commenting to one of my better friends in the class that those were really nice people in high school were still just as nice. I then commented to him that sadly, the assholes were still just that, referring to Kizer. He laughed and agreed with the assessment.

My dad had taught us kids how to deal with idiots like Kizer. Dad taught us a poem that I'm sure most readers will be familiar with. It went like this, "Sticks and stones may break my bones, but names will never harm me." Dad also said people who make fun of others do so because there's something about themselves and their life they're not happy about. He also told me it was the same with bullies who like to pick on people because it gave them the sense they were tougher and better than the others. Dad said it was merely their lack of self-confidence and positive self-image that was the problem.

My first learning opportunity with martial arts came from the husband of our neighbor's daughter. He was a paratrooper in the US Army. Under him, I began studying different judo/jujitsu throws and striking techniques. This didn't last long because he wasn't in town long. Being deployed to different overseas locations made it difficult for him to spend much time with his in-laws.

I did manage to find different books at the local library on martial arts subjects like judo, karate, and jujitsu, all written by a guy named Bruce Tegner. I would study the pictures and read the instructional pages, soaking up every word and picture. I always wondered how this guy had become such an expert on so many of these different fighting arts. During my junior and senior years, I was able to join a Korean karate club at Vincennes University (VU). The instructor, Dennis Callahan, had recently been discharged from the US Air Force. While stationed in Korea, Dennis had earned his black belt. After enrolling at VU, he had started the club. More on my martial arts endeavors and background later.

I had always wondered how effective the techniques and tactics I was studying in self-defense were. One day during my sophomore year, a guy I knew named John came to visit me. He'd brought a friend of his with him. I didn't know the guy and didn't remember seeing him around our school. John had been telling this friend of his about my martial arts training. John's friend seemed skeptical and asked me challenging questions. Finally, he asked me about being able to defend against a knife attack. My response was to run if I could; otherwise, stand and defend myself. He continued to press the issue about how I would do that. Finally, out of nowhere, he produced a pocket knife and what I'd do if he came at me. I'd hardly began to explain when he lunged forward, extending the hand with the knife. Mind you, the knife was open, and he didn't appear to be playing. I stepped to my left, deflecting his right hand with my left hand while simultaneously striking him across the bridge of his nose and underneath his right eye with the knife edge of my right hand. He dropped the knife as he cried out and grabbed his face, dropping down to one knee. There was a bit of blood, which we managed to stop. John was staring wide-eyed at his friend and asked him why he'd done that. His friend responded, saying he didn't believed me or in the martial arts training I was involved in.

After getting John's friend cleaned and patched up, they left. When I returned to school several days later, I sensed a difference in the way some treated me. Where some in the "in crowd" had mocked me with the Tarzan or Naz nickname, like Kizer, they now appeared to be a bit more reverent and polite. I never heard anyone mention or refer to that incident in my basement, not even John. Yet I couldn't help but feel they knew. As for me, my wondering about the effectiveness of my training had been answered unequivocally.

During the summers of 1963, '64, and '65, Mom had enrolled Steve and me in summer camp at Culver Military Academy. Steve only completed that first summer. It really wasn't his cup of tea, even though as a horse lover, he was able to ride with the Black Horse Troop. Probably living in troop tents with no air-conditioning, wearing a uniform, and having to march to meals, as well as participate in parades, didn't appeal to him

Culver is located on the north shores of Lake Maxinkuckee in Northern Indiana, just south of Plymouth. The lake is naturally spring-fed and measured a mile and a half east to west and two and a half miles north to south. The summer camp lasted eight weeks. My first summer in Naval Company 1 was an eye-opener.

I was a newly registered third-class midshipman that first summer. I had to learn to make square corner beds, fold my close around six and four-inch cardboards so everything was uniformed on the shelves, and hang my clothes facing all the same direction, spaced equally apart, with all buttons buttoned, zippers zipped, and no cables (strings or threads) or labels to be found anywhere. Those of us who been through military boot camp know this all too well. There may be some slight difference, but the similarities are still there.

I don't recall the name of my roommate that first summer. During my second and third summers at Culver, my roommate was Jose Alfonso Bonilla Pedroza. His nickname was Pepe, and he came from Torreon, Coahuila, Mexico. Neither one of us spoke the other's language. It made for an interesting summer. I spent a lot of time with Pepe and several of the other Latin American midshipmen. Some of them were from Mexico and other Central and South American countries.

They helped me develop the proper accent when I spoke Spanish and taught me all the best cusswords and phrases. I guess those are the words many of us learn before really beginning to speak our new language properly.

After finishing my third summer at Culver, I graduated as a first classman. I didn't accomplish any rank per se, nor did I occupy any important positions. Here again, I wasn't the most stellar of students. I could make a great bed and march with the best of them though.

Jose and I lost contact with each other until 2018. I had contacted Culver back in 1999, asking them if they had an address for Jose. They sent me an email with what they believed was his most current one. It wasn't until 2018, while cleaning my desk in my den, that I came across the email. I wondered if he might be on Facebook, so I checked. Sure enough, I found him and made contact. When we last saw each other, I could barely speak his language. I'm sure he was surprised when we made contact and it was all in Spanish. Our hope is to meet somewhere in 2019 or 2020 for a reunion. We've got over fifty years of catching up to do.

After graduating from Lincoln High School in May of 1966, Mom moved Steve, Sue Ellen, and me back to Indianapolis, Indiana. I spent the summer working at Sears in their sporting goods department and training in Ishinryu (Okinawan Ishinryu karate) at Clearance Ewing's dojo on Washington Street. I earned my green belt before leaving for the military.

Mom asked me what I was going to do about the draft. During the sixties, the military draft was in effect because of Vietnam. Those high school graduates who did not attend a college or university could expect to be drafted into the United States Army. With my grades, college was definitely out of the question. I told Mom I was going to visit with the recruiters of the different branches of the military and see what they might have to offer.

At this point it's important to understand the era in which all of this was taking place. It was the height of the Cold War between the USA and Russia. During school we had civil defense drills where we were required to hide under our desks. That's right, under the desks in our school classrooms. Like that would protect us from a nuclear blast.

Khrushchev was seen on TV pounding his shoe on the table during a United Nations meeting saying, "we don't have to invade you. We'll destroy you from within." While Russia is no longer a super power and the cold war ended in 1993, his admonition still holds true. Why you ask? Because of the growing number of socialist and communist who occupy positions in congress and other places in our institutions of higher education.

Also playing out on our TVs and in the news was the Cuban Missile crisis of 1962. From October 16–28, 1962, America was in a standoff with Russia because the American government had discovered the Soviets were working with the Cuban's to place ballistic missiles on the Cuban island ninety miles from the shores of Florida. The movie, "Thirteen Days," chronicles President Kennedy's struggles with the situation and the decisions he had to make. It was scary time for all Americans. Over all these years the Russians have changed little. They still like to rattle their sabers and cause the US

44

problems on the global stage. What has also changed little is the level of appeasement the Democratic Party has when dealing with them.

These were real events that happened during a time when there was the ever present threat of nuclear war. It wasn't a skit on Saturday Night Live, or some other comedy. It was the real world of that day. For this reason primarily, I see people on the left as those who were silently or not so silently supporting communist encroachments and takeover attempts in Central and South America.

Fast forward to the middle 1980's when the Iran-Contra scandal was in full swing and you'll find the Democratic control congress passing laws to ensure the Reagan administration could not support those forces fighting communist led rebellions. It's sad to say. But throughout my life, especially the last few decades, democrats have been more interested in supporting leaders and countries that were heavily socialistic or outright communist. Such have been the loyalties of leftists in this country for decades. These are also the same folks who hold no religious beliefs what so ever.

Another aspect of this era was the ongoing battle with race relations. I remember watching television and seeing then governor of Alabama George Wallace (a Democrat) standing on the steps of the high school in Montgomery to keep blacks from being integrated with the whites. This is also the time frame with Martin Luther King marched in his effort to bring about equal treatment for blacks before his assassination in April of 1968. That was a few short years after President John Kennedy was killed in Dallas in November of 1963, and a couple of months before President Kennedy's brother Robert was murdered in June of 68.

Add to this the affects the war in Vietnam was having and you have time during American history when protests were taking place on a regular basis. And students in various colleges and universities were very enamored with communism and wanted to change American into a more socialistic/communistic society.

Joining the Military

I ended up joining the US Air Force. I thought I might be able to get training in a career that would benefit me after I completed my four-year tour of duty for Uncle Sam. After reporting for induction to the recruiting center in Indianapolis in October of 1966, I was transported to San Antonio, Texas, and Lackland Air Force Base (AFB).

We arrived at Lackland after several hours of flying. We first flew from Indianapolis to Dallas. Then after changing from a jet to a propeller-driven aircraft, we finished our journey to San Antonio. It was around 2:00 a.m. when we arrived at the base and were ushered off the bus by the booming voices of our drill instructors. Yup, this ain't Indiana anymore, Mike, me boy.

We got to sleep shortly after that only to be awakened a few short hours later by the loud booming voices of our drill instructors as they beat on trash cans with sticks. Tech Sergeant Upchurch was our head drill instructor. He gave all of us the impression he took no prisoners and ate little boys for breakfast. After that, it was off to the indoctrination center (known as the green monster) for our introduction into the US Air Force and our new lives. Here we underwent more physical exams, received immunization shots, were issued our uniforms and boots and so on. By the time we finished, we were each carrying large duffle bags over our shoulders as we marched back to our barracks.

The barracks was a two story wood structure that dated back to World War II, if not more. On both levels there were two rows of beds. The first bed in the row was a single, followed by a line of bunk beds. The floor was a highly polished wood. I found out later why it

was so shiny. Every week those who resided on each floor moved all
of the beds and lockers outside. The floor was then stripped, cleaned
and re-waxed. The waxing process was a line of guys stretching from
one wall to the opposite wall spreading canned wax along the floor
as we backed our way towards the rear exit. Once the wax was dry
we started the buffing process in the same line formation at the rear
exit area moving towards the front entry. It was a long process that
resulted in some beautifully shined floors.

During the start of the second week, we were taken to a classroom and told to make our top three choices for the job we would
like to do in the Air Force. We were given a handbook containing
all the Air Force Specialty Codes (AFSCs). Each code provided a
description of what that career was all about. After looking through
it for a few minutes, I came upon, "radio intercept analysis specialist." That sounded really high speed, so I put that as my first choice.
The second choice was for air police (the title change that very year
to security police), and the third choice was medic. I figured the last
two were no-brainers since they always needed cops and medics.

In the second to the last week of our six weeks of basic training,
we began receiving our orders. Many of the guys were heading off to
tech schools to learn their new trade. I ended up with an assignment
to Sheppard AFB. I was going direct duty (meaning no tech school)
to a base supply job as a first level. I confronted TSgt Upchurch and
was told Uncle Sam would put me where he needed me most. I wonder to this day why they wasted time letting us think we had a choice.

As a nineteen-year-old small-town Midwesterner at Sheppard, I
began learning about supply. This covered everything from small bin
storage to outside bulk storage and warehousing. I learned to drive
forklifts and various sizes of trucks. I was also taught how to ship
and receive a variety of different types of supplies and equipment. In
addition to the hands-on training I was receiving, I was studying so
I could test and upgrade my job knowledge in order to move from a
first level to a third level. This set the stage for my promotion from
E-2 to E-3, or airman first class. The extra pay was great. After that,
my studies focused on the next marker, which was the fifth level and
the ability to promote to the next two ranks.

Christmas and New Year's Day of 1966 at Sheppard was the loneliest time I'd ever spent anywhere. I didn't know very many people. Those who did know me saw me more as loner and not someone they wanted to hang out with. I didn't always want to hang out with some of them anyway because of the things they liked to do. If I wasn't comfortable in a group or with what was happening, I'd leave. I found by keeping to myself, I could focus on other interests. That turned out to be my karate training. Since I couldn't find anyone to train with at first, I started classes at the local YMCA. That really helped to pass the time.

During my assignment at Sheppard, I continued to train in Korean karate under Technical Sergeant (TSgt) Allen. I was also able to participate in two tournaments. The first one was at Fort Bliss in El Paso, Texas, in August of 1967. The competition was billed as the First Armed Forces Karate Tournament. We spent several days training in the mornings and afternoons under the sharp eye and tutelage of Sensei Hidetaka Nishiyama. Sensei (meaning teacher in Japanese), as we referred to him, was the president of the Japanese Karate Federation in America, an internationally renowned teacher and author. He was from a direct lineage to O'Sensei Gichin Funakoshi, the founder of Shotokan Karate in Japan and the father of modern-day karate. At the end of the training days (five in all), a tournament was held.

As a brown belt, I competed with other brown and black belts in the same division. Such was the way competition was conducted in the Shotokan organization. My first match was also my last. The second the center referee started us off, we both threw right-leg roundhouse kicks and clashed shins in midair. The pain was excruciating. As a result, I was unable to continue and forced to forfeit.

The next year (1968) in May, the Second Armed Forces Karate Tournament was held at my base—Sheppard. This was the month before my fiancée Janie and I were scheduled to be married. Janie had never seen a karate tournament before. She had virtually no knowledge or understanding about the arts in general, or as a whole.

During the tournament, I put on breaking demonstrations. This included breaking cinder blocks (patio size 2" × 12" × 24") with my hand, elbow, or feet. Once the demonstrations were completed, the completion started. My match was the second one to take place. The guy I fought, an Army sergeant by the first name of Tom, was the same one who had won the tournament the year before. Tom was a second-degree (Dan) black belt who had been studying for ten years, of which five was in Japan. He was a strong, hard fighter. We fought the first regulation round, two overtimes, and a sudden death round before he beat me by one point. Because of my performance in the competition TSgt Allen promoted me to first-degree black belt.

While at Sheppard, I had also competed in Oklahoma City at a karate tournament run by Mr. Jack Hwang. Sun-seng-nim (Korean for *teacher*) Hwang was a well-known Korean instructor. He held tournaments during the year that were attended by people from several surrounding states as well as both coasts, Canada and Mexico. I competed as green belt in April of '67 and placed fourth in my division.

While stationed at Sheppard, I also began traveling to Dallas on weekends. I'd found a school run by Allen Steen on Mockingbird Lane. The school was run by a black belt instructor of Mr. Steen named Fred Wren. Fred was a tough instructor and always managed to hurt students he would spar with. Fred also became nationally recognized as a top competitor. I earned my brown belt from Mr. Steen in August of 1967.

While at Sheppard, I also learned about illegal drugs. Mind you, I was raised in a medical family. The only thing I knew about drugs were the ones the doctor prescribed for you or the ones your parents bought over the counter at the local drugstore.

As a single guy, I lived in the old World War II—style barracks that were located across the street from the Consolidated Mail Room I, or CMR I. My room was on the second floor. It was a corner room that looked out over the street and towards CMR I. Each of us was assigned duties in the barracks that involved cleaning the latrine (restrooms and showers) as well as mopping, waxing, and buffing the floor. Each airman and sergeant who resided in the barracks was also responsible for keeping his bed properly made and his floors spick-and-span. I got pretty good at buffing my floor and was awarded with a three-day pass on a couple of occasions having earned the "best room" title. Because I didn't have a roommate at first, keeping the room clean was easy. Once I had mopped and waxed the floors, I would buff them with an old piece of army blanket. The blanket would make the floor look like a mirror. The barracks sergeant once asked me what my secret was. I just smiled.

During this part of my life, I smoked cigarettes. I'd started just before beginning my freshman year of high school. By the time I got to Sheppard. I was smoking from two to two and a half packs a day. At $.25 a pack, or $5 a carton, it wasn't as expensive as it is today. I would periodically come into the barracks after work or on weekend and smell what seemed like burning grass. Like someone had raked the yard and set it on fire. I finally found out it was another airman who worked elsewhere on the base who smoked a pipe. I asked him why he smoked that foul-smelling stuff. Why didn't he smoke regular pipe tobacco? He told me while this didn't smell all that good, he liked it. He asked me to try a little. After a couple of puffs, I started to feel nauseated and began coughing. After everyone had a good laugh at my expense, I commented on how nasty I thought his tobacco tasted.

A few days later, I came into the barracks just as the security police were taking this guy out in handcuffs. I asked one of the other guys what was going on. They told me the stuff he was smoking in his pipe was marijuana, an illegal drug. I explained that I didn't know what that was. My fellow airman and barracks mates asked me where I was from, almost like they thought I was from another planet. I explained I was from Indiana. One of them asked me why I didn't know about drugs like that. I explained that the only drugs I knew about were the ones a doctor prescribed. I later found out the guy arrested was from California.

Where I was raised, being risqué was swimming naked in the striper pits (stone quarry), getting someone over twenty-one to buy you alcohol (beer or a pint of something), or sneaking friends into the drive-in theater in the trunk of your car. Drugs like marijuana, heroin, or cocaine were not known to me until then. I guess growing up in a small town in southwestern Indiana had its benefits. I wasn't exposed to drugs of that nature or the kind of lifestyle my California barracks buddy had come from. I was spared having those kinds of challenges confront me when I was younger. Now at nearly twenty, those things didn't appeal to me because I knew using them was both wrong and dangerous.

While at Sheppard, some of the friends I'd made during my assignment there approached me about driving to Denton, Texas, where there was an all-girls university. This included my new roommate Pete Proctor. Pete was another Hoosier. He was brought up in Fort Wayne, Indiana. Since none of them had a car, I was their best friend. I checked the map to see where Texas Woman's University (TWU) and Denton were from Wichita Falls in North Texas on the Oklahoma and Texas state line. I found that one-way travel was a hundred miles.

At the next meeting of our little group, I told them I hadn't lost anything in Denton and didn't see why I needed to go there. After some serious cussing and discussing, I gave in. They agreed to pay for the gas, food, and lodging. All I had to do was drive. I guess it was better than hanging around Wichita Falls and fighting with the townies (local guys) who weren't real fond of the GIs on the base.

At the close of business that Friday in August of 1967, we had the car packed and set off for Denton. When we arrived at the campus, we saw an abundance of pretty young ladies walking the sidewalks of the dorm area. After that first visit, we returned every weekend we could, depending on duties. We were like Muslims returning to Mecca. It was during one of the weekend visits I saw the girl who would later become my wife.

The first time I laid eyes on Maria Juanita Lara, she was walking along the sidewalk by the dorms wearing a miniskirt with the fishnet hose, a purse dangling from her shoulder, and just over-shoulder-length straight dark hair. At five feet tall, Janie (as she preferred to be called) was a petite young lady who caused guys' heads to turn at the sight of her. Such was the beauty of this young woman. As my fellow airman and I continued returning to TWU on weekends, I kept looking for a way to get an introduction to her. I hoped I'd see her with friends I knew who could introduce us. She doesn't remember that first meeting. I guess I didn't make much of an impression.

The second meeting happened while I was on a date with one of her friends—clearly, not the best timing on my part.

On the third occasion, one o'clock in the afternoon of January 13, 1968, in the TWU Student Union building basement where the snack bar was located, I saw her sitting at a table with two other girls I knew. I proceeded to approach the table and sat down. I said hello to my friends and heard Janie say in Spanish, "Who does this gringo think he is, sitting down without permission?" The girls quickly tried to silence her by telling her I understood Spanish. Truth be known, my Spanish abilities weren't that great. But the stage was set. She told me to play some music on the jukebox on the other side of the room. I went over to it and put in twenty-five cents and search for some good songs. In those days, a quarter would allow you to play six songs. When I returned to the table after choosing the songs, Janie looked at me and said, "You back already?" in a somewhat dismissive manner.

Later, we went for a drive. She and three of her girlfriends joined me in my 1960 Chevy Impala convertible. I conveniently arranged for her to sit in the middle next to me. After driving around for a while, we stopped at the car wash. While I was washing the car, she started it and acted like she was going to drive off. I opened the hood and pulled the distributor wire, shutting off the engine. When I reconnected everything in preparation to leave, the car won't start because the distributor had gotten wet. The back-and-forth jousting with Janie that afternoon was nonstop. Not only was she beautiful, she was also feisty and had a great sense of humor. Little did I know what God had planned for us.

I asked her out on a date to the movies later that afternoon. She told me she didn't date guys who smoked. So, here I was smoking around two and a half packs of Winston's a day. I took the half pack that was in my shirt pocket out, wadded it up, and threw it away. I told her I no longer was a smoker. We had our first date that night, and I haven't smoked a cigarette since. It wasn't until later in life I realized what a huge favor she'd done for me. Those who smoked were found to be at very high risk for developing lung cancer.

Over the next several months, I came to know the beauty of her personality, her sense of humor, and her generosity for others and life in general. Even though she was beauty-queen gorgeous, she was never stuck up or conceited. She looked for the best in others and had a keen sense for those who were out to take advantage of others.

The first time I ask Janie to marry me she called and talked with her parents. Her dad said absolutely not. When she told her mother I was trying to convince her to elope, her mom took the bus from Raymondville to Denton. That was easily a twelve hour trip with all the stops along the way. I got to know her mom over the next twenty-four hours. I don't know what transpired between her and Janie's dad when she got home, but we got the green light to get married.

Five months after asking her out on our first date, Janie and I were married in Raymondville, Texas. I'd told her if she married me, I'd show her the world. With orders to Spain, I was off to a good start. I hadn't realized it at that time, but I had found my soul mate. I have been forever grateful to my Heavenly Father for this wonderful blessing. Not only had God placed her in my life, but He had provided a person who would also be a guide for me in the decisions and direction we would take over the next fifty years.

Janie and me at Texas Women's University in Denton, Texas in the Spring of 1968. During the time we were dating

Our marriage was a traditional Catholic Mexican one. The priest, during our pre-wedding meetings, talked with us about our goals and background. Since I was a Protestant (Lutheran/Presbyterian), he told me he would not ask me to promise raising our children as Catholics. His only request was we promise to raise them as Christians. To this day I have a tremendous respect for the man and his approach with promoting Christianity.

My father- and mother-in-law, Celilio and Francisca Lara Sr., were both from the Mexican village of Matewala, in the state of San Luis Potosi. They had migrated to the southern part of Texas during the middle 1940s. All their children were born and raised as proud Americans. Janie had two older brothers, Ray and Felipe, who both served in the military during Vietnam. Cecilio Jr. and Robert, the two younger boys, were both still in high school. Mom and Dad spoke very little English. When Janie and I returned from our assignment in Spain, I was able to converse with them much better.

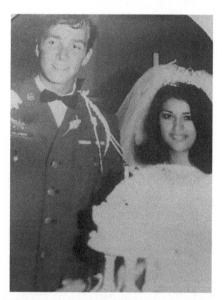

This is a picture of Janie and me at our
wedding reception on June 1968

Dad was a laborer and worked for the cotton gin companies that flourish here in South Texas. Mom was a housekeeper and worked for a local Anglo family in Raymondville. Dad was quiet and a hard worker. Mom was the banker of the family and had a strong entrepreneurial spirit. Through hard work and frugal handling of funds, she was able to help some of her sons attend college.

When Janie and I left for Indiana in May of 1972, we gave Mom a 1965 Plymouth Valiant four-door sedan. When we returned two years later, she had taught herself how to drive and taken on an Avon route. Over the years, Mom saved her money and eventually had purchased four rental properties. Today, she's ninety-three and living with dementia in an assisted-living home not far from us. She has regular visits from family members. When things got tough, Janie suggested to Mom she should seek government assistance. Mom refused. She said she'd made it all these years without any handouts, and she wasn't about to start now.

My First Overseas Assignment

I continued my military service at our new assignment in Spain. After taking our vows on June 15 of 1968 in Raymondville, Texas, we drove to Indiana to meet my family for a short two-week honeymoon. After the two week vacation I reported to my new duty station, Base Air Morón de la Frontera on July 11 of that same year. The base was located some fifty-five kilometers outside of Seville, Spain, which is located in the southern province of Andalucía. Janie joined me that September. We found a furnished apartment and began our new lives together.

I was also entering a new chapter in my life. This was a chapter that began to open my eyes about the Hispanic culture. Sure, my Latin buddies at Culver had started the ball rolling, but this was living full-time with my new wife whose first language was Spanish and who had been raised her whole life in the Mexican culture. Also partly because we were going to be living in Spain for two years, but mainly because I had become part of a Mexican American family. I joked with friends about it being a good thing we were starting our lives together in Spain. If she were to get mad at me, it was too far for her to row home to Mom.

I found a local judo club and came to terms with its owner for me to teach classes on Tuesday and Thursday evenings. My Spanish was not good enough to teach the class in a manner that would allow me to fully explain the techniques and moves. I took a Spanish 101 class from the University of Maryland to help me understand grammar and conjugations. By the time Janie joined me September of that year (1968), I was doing much better. The class quickly filled up with both Spanish and American students.

Language, it would seem, was another one of those gifts God had blessed me with. Just one of the many blessings I made sure to take advantage of. Janie and I took the opportunity to travel and see Spain. On a trip to Madrid, I met two Korean martial arts instructors. They ran a traditional training hall (*dojang* in Korean) named Kim y Cho. The gym was located by the north train station in Madrid. I arranged to visit them every couple of months in order to train and continue learning more of the art of Tae Kwon Do. I would typically arrive early Saturday morning on the night train and go straight to the dojang.

The morning's training started with a run through the park that was adjacent to the school. We would run about two miles jumping over park benches and other obstacles. Occasionally, either Kim or Cho, depending who was leading the run, would suddenly reverse and begin attacking the line of students, about twelve to fourteen in all. After his attack, the next in line would follow suit until the instructor was back in front of the line.

Over the next eighteen or so months, I would study the forms (kata or poomsae) while in Sevilla from General Che Hong Hi's book on Tae Kwon Do. When I visited Kim and Cho, they would correct my movements and teach me more. It was a slow and tedious process. I'd read from the book and then perform the movements. Over time, I would have the whole form down and move on to the next one.

Also over the two years we were stationed in Sevilla, we enjoyed taking strolls down the many historic streets of old Sevilla, walking past the bullfighting stadium and the Torre del Oro by the Hotel Luz de Sevilla. We also enjoyed shopping at the Galaria department store and going *tasca*-hopping in the evenings. Tascas were small servings of food you could buy at a bar, along with a *cana* (small glass of beer). Over the process of visiting several bars, you ended up having consumed your evening meal. Walking throughout this process also helped to minimize the alcohols effect. We have some wonderful memories of those days.

Key among those memories was the March/April time frames. During March, there was a two-week time frame when Semana Santa (Saint's Week) processions were held. Each of the small Catholic churches would carry the heavy platforms that held either a statue of Christ or the Virgin Mary. This possession would travel the streets of Sevilla until they arrived at the main cathedral where the statue would be blessed by the head priest. Then the process would reverse itself until the statue and those carrying it had returned to their home church. What we found interesting about this was the reason each person under the platform had taken on the burden and responsibility to carry this heavy object. It was part of a penance for some sin they had confessed and were required to do as a result.

During this time of religious practice of prayers and processions, no one would eat during the daytime. Once the evening had settled in and everyone had returned home, then it was time for their meal. Those who marched in the processions were dressed in either white or black robes with tall pointy hats that dropped down to the shoulders with opening for the eyes that gave us as Americans the impression we were witnessing the KKK marching on the streets. It was truly a learning experience for the two of us.

In April, after all the solemnest and piety of the Semana Santa days, the Feria de Abril (April Fair) would begin. This was a time of some ten days or so of merriment and partying. Families and companies would set up *casetas* (tents) where family and friends would come to drink wine and eat till they were ready to explode. This was Spain's version of Oktoberfest. Having lived in Germany and Spain, I can tell you both countries know how to have a good time.

By the time Janie and I finished our tour of duty in Spain, I'd earned my second-degree black belt. Upon returning to the USA, I was discharged, and we joined my mother in Indianapolis for some rest and relaxation. After several months in Indiana, which included attempting to open a karate school in South Bend with my former instructor Dennis Callahan, Janie and I headed south to her parents' home in Raymondville Texas.

Becoming a College Student and Police Officer

As I've previously stated, I was raised in small-town USA. Growing up in a Southern Indiana town of around twenty thousand, I only knew about three ethnic groups. These groups were whites, blacks, and Orientals. Hispanics were considered to be part of the white group, as were Italians and other Mediterranean peoples. When we moved to the Rio Grande Valley of South Texas after leaving the Air Force, and some vacation time at Mom's place in Indianapolis, I got a whole new education. In this area, the relations between whites and Mexicans (as most referred to them) were not good.

Many of the whites of South Texas had abused and taken advantage of these people, much in the same way whites had discriminated and taken advantage of the blacks for decades. Many of the Caucasians who had lived their lives in South Texas had an arrogant and condescending attitude toward them. When Janie and I would go places, I would hear the Chicanos (a title that had been adopted by Mexican Americans as a way to single them out from other Hispanics) comment in Spanish that they thought whites should stay with their own kind. They didn't like seeing a Chicana (Janie) with a gringo (me). They didn't know we were married and had no idea I spoke fluent Spanish. This reminded me of the same things I'd hear white folks say when they saw a white girl with a black man.

Janie and me at a restaurant that featured
flamingo dancing in Seville Spain

The picture I was getting about the relationships between whites and Hispanics along the border was a negative one. I felt embarrassed that my race was so disrespectful and demeaning to them in the same way they'd been towards blacks for decades. One example was the day I'd applied to be a police officer in Alamo, Texas, a small community of around twelve thousand. After picking up an application, I was walking toward my car. A couple of Anglos who were volunteer fire firefighters and present in the office when I asked for the application, said, "You don't want to work with this police department." I asked them why. They said, "Because they're all Mexican." Without hesitation, I said, "What makes you think I'm not?" They looked at each other and headed off in a different direction.

It was no different than the way whites had treated blacks in other parts of the country for decades. Here again, I'm ashamed of my own race because of the arrogant attitudes of superiority they've had—and still have in some quarters—over minorities. What's even sadder for me is many of these white people claim to be Christians. If that were the case, they were devoid of the true love Christ taught his disciples while he was on earth and, even to this day, encourages us to practice the New Testament. We are all God's children, regardless of ethnicity or color.

On a vacation with the family when I was around eight or nine, we drove down from Indiana to Florida. Along the way, I remember stopping at places to gas up the car or get some food. I also remember seeing restrooms and water fountains that were labeled whites only or blacks only. I asked Mom and Dad why they were separated like that. Dad told me it was because a lot of whites in the southeastern part of our country had been treating black people as slaves and second-class citizens. He told me I would learn about those things as I continued my education. He said there are some of our leaders who are trying to fix that problem.

I started my freshman year at Pan American University in the fall of 1971. Pan Am, as it was known, later became University of Texas—Pan American (or UT Pan American) when the school was assimilated into the UT system. I also started working as a police officer in Raymondville. I felt this would give me the theory on one hand and the reality on the other. During this time in Texas, a person could work as a police officer for up to twelve months before going to a police academy. Add to this the federal government had established a program to help cities and towns add more police officer to their respective departments.

This program was known as the Law Enforcement Assistance Program or LEAP. A city could hire a new officer who would be paid by the feds for a year. Since they didn't have to send the new officer to an academy right away (they had twelve months), they worked them for a year and let them go. Such was the way things went for me. My monthly pay during this period was a whopping $305 a month—before taxes.

This was my first experience with being a police officer. As the months went by, I began learning about small-town politics. I didn't like what I was seeing or experiencing. The city fathers, as they were referred to (the mayor and city commissioners), would have us downgrade arrests. One man I arrested for driving while intoxicated (DWI) later had his charges reduced to public intoxication.

These politicians also involved themselves in running the police department, in some cases overriding decision the chief would make. I know he was frustrated. They'd hired him to run the department because of his background and experience. Now they were telling him how to do his job.

Later in April of 1972, as my second semester at the university was coming to a close, I wrote a letter of recognition to the chief, the city commissioners, and the mayor. I told them how disappointed I was in their complete lack of care regarding their police department. When I was hired, I received a badge and two shirts with patches. Everything else I had to purchase out of pocket. The department's patrol car was a Plymouth Fury I with a three speed-standard shift on the steering column. The car had no-air conditioning and could even catch a Volkswagen beetle. The chief was usually drunk and was unable to talk with his officers regarding discipline issues without his son by his side. Some of the officers were so fat they couldn't get out of the patrol car very easily. God forbid they'd have to run after someone. It was a hell of a way to begin my law enforcement career.

While going to Pan Am and working as a cop, I also started a karate club on campus. While stationed at Shepard AFB, I had begun teaching karate classes at the local YMCA in February of 1967 as a brown belt. Among some of my students were police officers. I learned that teaching cops was different than teaching civilians. This was because of the requirement for police to follow a graduated use of force policy. Where a civilian could defend themselves until the attacker ceased to be a threat, a police officer has to explain in his report what the subject did that required him to use the force and tactics he used. This was scrutinized by the officers' supervisors and the county's district attorney. Clearly, a tough standard applied to our law enforcement personnel.

After my freshman year, Janie and I packed up and moved back to Indiana. This was in May of 1972. My former karate instructor, Dennis Callahan, was starting a school in South Bend (again) and wanted me to be part of the instructional staff. Teaching karate full-time was one of my dreams. After arriving and settling in, I began working with Dennis and another one of his students, Mike Hurst. As time went along, it became clear this wasn't going to work.

I ended up finding other jobs in order to pay the bills. I sold insurance for John Hancock for a year. The boss wanted us to sell only whole life. Most of the people I would try and help could only afford term insurance. Since term insurance doesn't pay as much into the organization, the boss would always get upset. I did what I felt was right.

After leaving John Hancock, I drove for Allied Van Lines until I failed to see a low bridge sign and damaged a trailer. They had to let the air out of the back set of tires on the tractor in order to back the truck out from under the bridge. My boss told me he could no longer employ me because his insurance company would not cover me anymore. He told me he hated to lose me since I was really good at packing furniture and boxes in the trailers for moving. The furniture I'd packed in southern Ohio was undamaged, even though the roof of the trailer was peeled back like a sardine can. In reality, I didn't miss the hard work of moving furniture. Just try hauling a sleep couch up a flight of stairs to the second floor. UGH!

Next, I went to work with a construction company that had a contract with the Michigan City State Prison. The contract involved replacing the underground piping throughout the prison. Some of the pipes we dug up were very old wooden water mains that dated back to the 1800s. These old-style water pipes had an outside diameter of around fifteen inches, with a four-inch hole down the center. They were created by taking a large tree trunk and cutting it down the middle. Then the center was hollowed out to create the four-inch main after the two halves were reunited. The halves were banded together and the whole piece covered in tar. Once they were in place and water ran through them, the wood would expand, sealing itself. I found this example of early engineering fascinating.

Working in the prison was also an experience. The guards kept a wary eye on us and the prisoners walking around in the yard area where we were working. The guards gave us a tour of the death penalty room where the electric chair sat. Named Old Sparky by the guards, it was a massive solid wooden thing, much like you saw if you watched the movie the *Green Mile*.

My main job was to drive the dump truck taking the dirt out of the prison as the trenching was being done. Later, I would bring dirt back in when they were ready to fill the trenches back up. Many times, we dug dirt up in one area and put it an area we'd finished working in. I would also work down in the trench, loosening dirt or using the jackhammer to break up cement. That aspect of the job proved to be dangerous. On more than one occasion, one of the side walls collapsed, trapping one or more of the workers. We had to scramble to uncover them. I missed being one of those guys by very little a couple of times. This provided for some very tense and scary moments.

One afternoon while I was standing by the truck, a guard came over and told me to stay clear. He and a couple other guards were going to do a search of an inmate they'd been told had a weapon on him. I made sure to stay several yards away as they confronted the man. As they began patting him down, he suddenly broke free and pulled a long black object from inside his shirt. During the struggle, one of the guards was cut on the hand. The prisoner was subdued, placed in handcuffs, and taken away.

One of the guards came over to me and showed me the weapon they'd retrieved. It was a solid metal file that had been ground down on both edges, forming a point in one end. In effect, it was a dou-ble-edged dagger. This was my first experience inside a state prison where I was able to observe prisoner conduct and attitudes up close. These were clearly people you wouldn't want as neighbors.

Also during the time we were in South Bend, I had located a place and began running my own karate school. Since the efforts to start and run one with Callahan and Hurst, I decided to try it by myself. After working all day, I would go to the school and teach. The school was located in the downtown area of South Bend in what was once a car dealership.

In the beginning, I had to paint, clean, and fix the place up so it was presentable for the classes. Over time, the school took on a more professional look. Even so, Janie pointed out we weren't getting very far, and I should reconsider going back to school. My wife's wisdom proved to be right on the mark. In July of 1974, we headed back to South Texas.

When we returned, I started my sophomore year. It was the fall of 1974. I'd gone back to work in law enforcement with the Willacy County Sheriff's Department as a jailer and dispatcher. Because of the letter I'd written before leaving for Indiana in April of '72, I was not very welcome among some of the city fathers. In hindsight, my overzealousness to point out the city's police department problems and failures should have been kept to myself. This was one of my many learning experiences about why hindsight was 20/20.

Janie had gone to work with Bealle's Department store in Edinburg, Texas. This is the same city where the UT Pan American is located. We'd found a two-bedroom duplex a few blocks from the university. This allowed me to ride my bike to and from the campus, saving gas.

I'd also rekindled my karate classes. One of my former students from the 1971–72 time frame approached me about helping the Air Force ROTC detachment with a project they were working on. They wanted to run a karate tournament in order to earn money that would be used to offset the cost of a Dinning In that was to be held that December. A Dinning In was a formal dinner where all the detachments staff and cadets would attend. It was also during this dinner awards would be handed out.

I went to the first meeting and listened to the plans they'd set up for their tournament. I advised them they would end up losing money for a variety of reasons. The assistant professor of aerospace instructions, Major Stockton, asked me if I'd be willing to help. I became their de facto director/promoter.

After setting up committees to handle different aspects of the planning, promoting, and running of the tournament, the major told me he thought I had pretty good leadership skills. He asked me if I'd be interested in joining the Air Force. I laughed and told him I'd been there and done that already. After explaining, he asked me again if I'd be interested in becoming an officer in the Air Force. I told him I needed to confer with my missus because we were a team and made important decisions together. After talking things over with Janie, I signed up. By the way, the karate tournament was a success and earned the detachment several hundreds of dollars. We held another one the following year that was equally successful.

In addition to keeping busy working and going to classes full-time and teaching karate classes again, I had to study and prepare for those classes. This included adding to my work load when I joined the Air Force ROTC. Where I had been carrying thirteen to fifteen credit hours per semester, I ended up with my last four semesters two with nineteen hours and two with twenty. Where my grades in elementary and high school were abysmal, to say the least, I managed to graduate with a low B average in December of 1976. Mind you, this was while still working as a full-time police officer while attending classes. The day after graduating, I was sworn back into the Air Force as a brand-new second lieutenant. Affectionately known as butter bars.

My mom was super proud of me and asked me what I would like as a graduation present. I told her the greatest gift she could give me would be to quit smoking. Mom and Dad had both quit smoking around the 1958–59 time frame. This was due to the medical information that was being published regarding smoking and lung cancer. Dad was able to quit cold turkey. My poor mom struggled for months. When Dad drowned, she started smoking again. That was July of 1962. Here I was, asking her to quit fourteen years later. To Mom's great credit, she did. There was no price tag you could have placed on that gift.

From the fall of 1971 until the late winter of 1976, I worked in three different cities (Raymondville, Mercedes, and Weslaco) in the Valley (short for Rio Grande Valley—this is how folks in South Texas referred to the area along the border with Mexico) as a patrolman. I had also worked with the Willacy County Sheriff's Department and as an investigator for the district attorney. Throughout these different positions and locations, I got to see the various neighborhoods and colonias (run-down residential areas, or slums as they would be referred to up north) on a daily basis. I responded to bar fights and domestic disturbances on a regular basis. I saw the rank poverty and a lack of education on the part of these people up close and in person almost daily. More than 85 percent of the verbal fights and arguments were in Spanish.

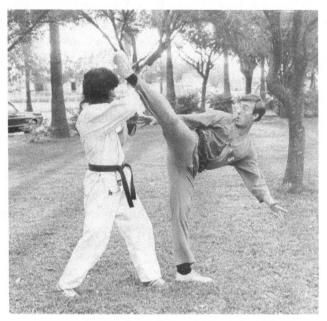

Me practicing kicks with my student Candelario
Arteaga in the city park in Edinburg, Texas where
I was teaching classes two days a week

A typical Friday night (and into the early morning of Saturday), we had to respond to residences because of fights between the husband and his wife. With far too much regularity, after the husband was paid on Fridays, he would make his way to the local cantina and drink with his friends until the closed the place. When he got home, his wife would get very mad at him for spending money on beer that was supposed to have been used to pay the bills and buy food. Mexican men didn't take kindly to their woman yelling at them— has everything to do with their machismo. This resulted in the wife being beaten up and occasionally having to be taken to the emergency room. The husband was wrestled to the ground (being drunk, they thought they could whip the world), handcuffed, and taken to jail. The children in the house grew up watching this theater play out far too often.

One must understand that Spanish spoken along the border between Mexico and Texas is not correct Castellano Spanish. Instead, it is often referred to as Spanglish. I know grown men with bachelors and master's degrees who can't conduct a conversation without bouncing back and forth between English and Spanish. Here's an example. "Es que [it's that] I don't really know what I'm going to do. Me intendes [do you understand]?" Or "Sabes que [you know what], I think I'll go to the store and buy some birunga [slang for beer]. Queres que te trigo un seis [you want me to bring you a six pack]?"

I've constantly come across people who've been living in this country for decades, both legally and illegally, who hardly speak a word of English. Oh, they get by with some rudimentary pigeon English. But they haven't made an effort to learn the language the entire time they've lived in our country. They've made no attempt to assimilate and become true Americans.

There have been countless occasions where people who'd come across the border (legally or illegally) to escape the violence, poverty, and lack of work over there, only to put up their Mexican flag on American soil. I always wondered why they didn't stay in their beloved Mexico and work to make it better. Clearly, their love was for Mexico, not the USA.

The only thing the USA offered was jobs. A great deal of the money these people made in their jobs in the USA was sent back home to their families in Mexico. I've heard discussion regarding why Mexico isn't keen on helping to enforce our immigration laws. According to sources, Mexico receives more than a billion dollars annually from expatriates working in America. Why would they want to change that?

Because of the language situation in Texas, non-Hispanic police officers who don't speak Spanish are at a great disadvantage. More than twenty years ago, in the Houston area, a six foot-four-inch constable was taken down and killed with his own gun by three small Mexicans. They talked to each other in Spanish, discussing how they would take him down, get his pistol away from him, and shoot him.

Since he didn't speak or understand any Spanish, he was clueless as to what was about to happen. Fortunately, the patrol car's dash cam caught the action, which included the license plate and facial images of the murderers. In today's police agencies, basic street Spanish is a requirement.

It was during the last couple of months working for the Weslaco Police Department before I resigned to leave for the Air Force that I was involved in my first hostage situation. The whole matter started with a husband-wife argument that ended with the husband firing off a small caliber semiautomatic into the ceiling of the home. The wife ran across the street and called the police, telling them he'd tried to kill her and that he was holding their children. I responded along with a number of other units.

Through negotiations back and forth with the man, we were able to convince him to put the pistol in his pocket. The officer talking with him had said to him he was afraid to come in to talk because he didn't want to get shot. The subject agreed to put the gun in his pocket in order for the officer to enter. While all this was taking place, I was standing to the side of the house with my .45 caliber 1911, pointing directly at him through a small crack in the curtains. It was during this hostage situation I was confronted for the first time with the question about taking a life.

As a Christian, I can tell you that is no small question to consider. I realized if this person attempted to harm in any manner another person with that gun, I would not hesitate to take him out. I had sworn an oath to enforce all laws—federal, state and local—and to protect life and property. I remember that day like it was yesterday. I give thanks to God to this day that I've never had to seriously injure or kill another human being during all the years I was in the military and as a police officer.

My Martial Arts Background

Throughout the previous pages, I've made reference to my efforts to study and train in the martial arts. What follows is a paper I wrote some years ago and have since updated. The paper provides a fairly complete picture of my martial arts training and studies. Wherever I've been stationed—here in the States or overseas in Europe—I've taught classes and participated in local martial arts training and competition. Since I have mentioned periodically this desire to learn and train in the martial arts, I felt it necessary to put it in perspective. Much of my personal beliefs, my personal bearing, my self-confidence, my code of conduct, my discipline and drive are the products of these efforts, coupled with my Christian education and beliefs over more than fifty-nine years. There is a strong corollary between the Christian teaching of respect and humility and those in traditional martial arts.

Decades of Martial Arts Training

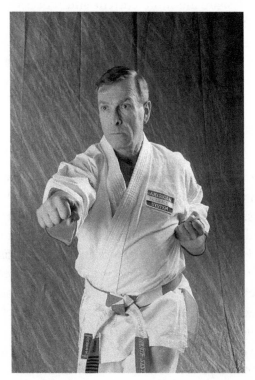

Me in a punching stance. This was used in
the AKS web site on my bio page

Preface

In March 1990, I submitted this paper to Mr. Lieb (our American Karate System [AKS] founder and chief instructor) in partial fulfillment of my sixth-degree black belt requirements. The points I made at that time are still relevant today. My friend and mentor suggested I update and share the paper with the American Karate System's membership, as well as other true students of the arts. I hope the thoughts and reflections that follow will have a positive impact on your personal perspective regarding the martial arts and your specific studies in karate. It is now March of 2019, and I'm updating this paper, so the comments I share are more current and reflective of who I am today at seventy-one. Remember, the comments and experiences I share below were written in March of 1990 and have recently been updated. I also ask your indulgence as there may also be some redundancy from previously described experiences.

Introduction

While talking with two of my newest students a few years ago, I discussed with them various experiences I'd had throughout my years in martial arts. I was attempting to help them understand certain techniques and movements I had worked hard to learn by myself, as well as others I had picked up from others of higher rank and several more years of training. What follows is my humble attempt to share my experiences and studies of martial arts over a period that covers nearly six decades. The purpose is to share as well as reflect on both the feelings and motivations that prompted me, and most people, to begin studying some form of the arts. As one's skill and awareness increase over a period of years, so also does one's philosophical perspective.

For purposes of this paper, the term *martial arts* will be used because of its all-encompassing definition. The more time people spend studying martial arts, the greater the chances they will, through the strains of both physical and mental endeavors, see the true essence of what it means to be one with the universe. I used the word *chances* because as with many things in life, the light fails to turn on for some people. That epiphany never happens. This could be due to no fault of their own or with the manner in which they trained. This understanding (or knowledge) is something that must be sought by people in their own way. The results they achieve or fail to achieve will be a manifestation of their own personal goals and efforts.

To further illustrate the point of enlightenment, the following quote from Shigeru Egami's book *The Way of Karate, Beyond Technique* is provided for your review. In the preface of his book, Egami discusses how the practice of karate has changed over the years with respect to technique, but not with respect to its ultimate goal:

> The ideal of Gichin Funakoshi, who has come to be recognized as the "Father of Karate-do" was to advance from jutsu (technique) to do (the way). It became my mission to realize this ideal, but here again, questions arise: What is the meaning of "from technique to the way"? Through what kind of practice can one attain this ideal? Karate-Jutsu or karate-do? The distinction between the two must be clearly grasped. Karate-Jutsu must be regarded as nothing more than a technique for homicide and that most emphatically, is not the objective of Karate-do. He who would follow the way of true karate must seek not only to coexist with his opponent but to achieve unity with him. There is no question of homicide, nor should emphasis ever be placed on winning. When practicing Karate-do, what is important is to be one with your partner, move together, and make progress together. (Pages 9 and 10)

An additional point required here is the difference between training and studying. Webster's II New Riverside University Dictionary defines the two words as follows: *Study:* "the act of studying; the pursuit of knowledge, as by reading, observation, or research." *Training:* (a) "to coach in or accustom to a mode of behavior or performance"; and (b) "to prepare physically, as with a regimen." I wish to point out the differences between these two words. In the beginning, we train. We are taught by an instructor who puts us through continuous physical exercises to develop our abilities to kick, block, punch, and move in the proper manner. When we arrive at a point where mere training is not satisfying our desire to learn, we begin to study. It is the combination of these two endeavors that bring the student of the martial arts to enlightenment. Also by studying the writings of various martial arts founders and masters, a person develops an even deeper understanding. Case in point is Funakoshi's second precept (of the twenty he espoused in Karate-do Niju kaju): "*Karate ni senti nashi* means there is no first strike in karate." What do you think Funakoshi meant by that?

In the Beginning

When I first became interested in learning the martial arts, it was purely for the selfish reason of being able to save my own bacon. If someone took a disliking to me and decided he wanted to beat me up, I wanted to have the capability to escape with minimal damage. As attempts at this had already occurred on several occasions, I was very motivated.

During the early 1960s, I lived in the small southwestern Indiana town of Vincennes where no classes in martial arts were available. I was able to talk to a neighbor's son-in-law, an Army paratrooper, into teaching me what he'd learned in the Army. I also worked hard at getting my hands on any and every piece of printed material about martial arts at our local library. As time went by, I came across one or two others who had received formal training in some form of martial art and persuaded them to teach me what they knew.

This went on until 1964, when the local junior college (Vincennes University) offered Tae Kwon Do classes. The classes were taught by a newly discharged airman who had finished his last tour of duty with the Air Force in Korea where he studied Chun Do Kwan Tae Soo Do and earned his first-degree black belt (first Dan). I joined the classes even though I was in high school. Many of the college students with whom I was training resented my presence. They attempted to get me to drop out by using both verbal and physical harassment. Of all the original students of that first class, I was the only one who continued to study and train in martial arts, eventually arriving at my present rank.

After graduating from high school and joining the United States' Air Force, I was stationed at Sheppard Air Force Base (AFB) in Wichita Falls, Texas, following my basic training in San Antonio's Lackland AFB. I continued my studies with Technical Sergeant Allen in the same system I had begun at the junior college, Chun Do Kwan Tae Soo Do. My first teacher, Mr. Dennis Callahan, had impressed upon me the need to avoid fighting whenever possible. If attempting to leave the scene to avoid trouble wasn't possible, his advice was to strike quickly and disappear. I observed him follow this philosophy at a dance one weekend at a club called Lamey's Lounge a few miles outside of Evansville, Indiana, on Highway 41. He had danced with a young lady who had a jealous boyfriend who found out what happened and came looking for Dennis. Dennis was unaware of what was going on until the boyfriend, accompanied by a small crowd of onlookers, confronted him. Dennis was unable to pacify the boyfriend because he had too many of his friends watching. When it became clear he wasn't going to talk his way out of a fight, Dennis hit the guy with a well-placed and well-controlled spear finger thrust in the throat. The irate boyfriend grabbed his throat, coughing and acting as though he had something lodged in it. During the confusion, Dennis and I slipped out and left the dance.

Sergeant Allen had a similar way of looking at things. He said, "If you get into a situation where you try your best to get away peacefully and it doesn't work, then the best defense is a good offense."

During the same time I was studying with Sergeant Allen, I also traveled on weekends to Dallas and trained at the Hillcrest Karate Institute owned by Allen Steen. The instructor in charge of the school was Fred Wren. This was my first occasion to come in contact with someone who truly enjoyed inflicting pain, or so it seemed to me at that time. Whenever Fred would demonstrate a technique, move, or free spar with one of the students, the student would invariably get hurt. Wren never displayed any remorse or concern. When I saw the movie *The Karate Kid,* the instructor who ran the Kobu Kai School and taught the students to "show no mercy," I was reminded of Fred Wren. I earned my brown belt from Mr. Steen in August of 1967.

Realization of Potential

I hadn't really come to appreciate the potential of what I'd been learning until an incident occurred during my vacation in the summer of 1967. While visiting my mother in Indianapolis, I went out for a hamburger with my brother and his friend. We went to a White Castle on Keystone and Thirty-Eighth Street where you could eat ten hamburgers for a dollar (very small hamburgers). When we pulled into the parking lot, we passed a car full of high school seniors celebrating their graduation. They didn't bother us when we went in, but when we came out, they began saying lots of dirty things about the military as I was in uniform. I told my brother and his friend to ignore them because nothing would be accomplished by fighting. As we began pulling out of the parking lot, a couple of them started kicking my car. That cut it! I stopped the car and told the other two to do their best. When I exited the car, there were three of them waiting for me. Their movements appeared to be in slow motion. When I hit them, it seemed as if I had barely touched them, even though they went down either screaming in pain or unconscious. We all took off when we heard the wail of police sirens in the distance. This event replayed in my mind's eye for months. I was amazed at what I'd been able to do and the effect of my actions. I can remember always wondering if the techniques I'd been learning were really effective. That evening's event put an end to my wonderings. There were no more doubts in my mind about the significance or effectiveness of what I was learning. It also brought to me a clear understanding of Funakoshi's second precept of Karate Ni Senti Nashi—there is no first strike in karate. Egami Sensei also quotes a similar comment by his teacher in his book where he points out that "there is no offense in karate" (Egami, *The Way of Karate, Beyond Technique*, p. 15). As a person advances in his abilities, he begins to see how to blend with the opponent rather than meeting them head-on. One can cause a great deal of damage by merely moving out of the path of an attacker and using the opponent's own momentum against him.

Continuing to Learn

My enlistment in the Air Force took me from Texas to southern Spain in the summer of 1968. In Spain, I started teaching at a judo school in the city of Sevilla (having earned my first-degree black belt that May), where my new bride, Janie, and I were renting an apartment. We'd gotten married just prior to departing for our new assignment. Other than judo, the people in Sevilla had had little to no exposure to any of the other martial art. Janie and I enjoyed traveling and seeing the sights. On our first trip to Madrid, I met Mr. Kim and Mr. Cho, two Koreans who ran their own karate school. I continued my studies with these two gentlemen during the few years we were stationed in Spain. I traveled to Madrid once every two months as time and money permitted. My training with them was tough. I usually arrived on a Friday and trained in the afternoon and evening. On Saturday at 6:00 a.m., some of the hardier students met at the school with one of the Korean instructors. We began running up the hill through the park, jumping over benches, and dodging each other as the front runner would turn and attack those behind him. Once he got to the end of the file, he would bring up the rear. This continued until the instructor was back in front again. After about two miles, we arrived back in the school parking lot where we formed a circle and began stretching. In this circle, we practiced various techniques and took turns in the middle, sparring with those who would attack us from different directions. I also attended an afternoon class and another in the evening that same day. Later that night, I would catch the train back to Sevilla. I would show up at work on Mondays, following a trip to Madrid with both of my shins and forearms covered in bruises. To this end, Sensei Egami states,

> In a sense, practice, whether done alone or in a group, is a battle against one's own self. There is a strong temptation to be lazy and practice leisurely. One should not be lazy; one should learn how to accept hard practice. One should not think of practice as a fight against an opponent. He should challenge the extreme limits of his own strength. (p. 108)

These two Koreans taught me how to develop a mental toughness I had previously not been forced to learn. They helped me see the abilities I had only previously believed others had. I remember Dennis Callahan once telling me when I had been trying to do a jump kick, "Elephants don't fly." Now, at five feet ten inches and two hundred pounds, I'm no lightweight. That doesn't mean it was impossible to learn how to do jump kicks if I put my mind to it. Through hard work and development of my muscles, as well as the appropriate mental outlook, I was able to realize some halfway-decent jump kicks. I was also able to become more flexible than I ever dreamed possible. This further helped to mold my mental attitude. The point is that a person's desire, mental openness, and attitude are the key factors between success and failure in life. After all, life is only a series of trial-and-error experiences that help us learn to deal with reality on a day-by-day basis. Likewise, the study of martial arts is the same. Only through experiencing and striving to learn the many techniques can we achieve the ability to progress up the ladder toward final success. Coupled with the forward movement toward success is the overall development of the person. This development, as Sensei Egami puts it, occurs at the same time. First, he says, "Beginning in the training of one's body, the practice continues with the training of one's spirit. Finally one realizes that body and spirit are not two things but one. This is true practice" (p. 15). Later, Sensei Egami states, "The body and spirit are fundamentally one.

If you train your body, your spirit will also be trained" (p. 100). As you can see, the importance of both physical and mental preparation will occur at the same time and are of equal importance toward one's overall development. It's also through these same efforts you begin to transition from mere training to study.

Tournaments

As a student of karate and an early subscriber of *Black Belt* magazine, I began my exposure to competition. My first tournament was in May 1966 at Jhonn Rhee's Nationals in Washington DC. I competed as an orange belt and won my first three matches. I believe this was also the tournament where Joe Lewis made his debut and won the black belt portion of the competition. There were some good fights and some bad ones. There was also good and bad judging. This resulted in several people getting their noses bloodied, teeth loosened or knocked out, and their faces cut, requiring stitches. During this period of karate competition, hand and foot protection, like the variety in use today, was nonexistent. Maybe Mr. Rhee realized a need for protective gear because of the injuries that occurred at his tournament. He invented the first pieces of safety equipment (1972/73) that spawned the industry that exists today providing competitors with a variety of hand, feet, head, and body gear they can wear to protect themselves.

As an enlisted man in the Air Force, I participated in one tournament as a green belt and two as a brown belt prior to going overseas to Spain. As a green belt, I participated in a tournament in Oklahoma City presented by the late Grandmaster Jack Hwang, a noted Korean instructor, and promoter. I won several matches at this competition and ended up in fourth place. As a brown belt, I competed in the first and second Armed Forces Karate Championships held at Fort Bliss in El Paso and Sheppard AFB in Texas respectively. In El Paso, I injured my right leg when an opponent and I clashed legs trying to execute the same kick. At the Sheppard AFB tournament, I fought the guy who'd taken first place in El Paso. The base newspaper talked about our match being one of the best of the entire event. We fought through regulation time, two overtimes, and finally, a sudden death, where he beat me by a point. I felt pretty good about this as he was a second-degree black belt who had studied for several years in Japan. I was only a first-grade brown belt. You may wonder why a brown belt would fight a black belt. The Japan Karate Association of America, headed by Hiditaka Nishiyama, ran the Armed Forces Tournaments. Their method of competition was to have brown and black belts fight in the same division. There were no separate divisions for brown and black belts. Sensei Nishiyama was a well-respected senior member of the Shotokan organization and former student of its founder, Gichin Funakoshi. It was after this tournament that Sergeant Allen promoted me to first-degree black belt (first Dan). Wow, what a feeling of accomplishment!

It may be helpful for the reader to understand the levels of rank used in various martial arts systems. When students begin their studies, they start at the tenth Kyu (grade) white-belt level. The progression upward varies depending on the style and/or school at which they study. As a rule, students move from white to yellow or orange, then green and blue, and finally brown (or red in some styles). In other words, the students start at the tenth Kyu level and reach the first Kyu level before becoming eligible for black-belt rank. Once a student earns his first Dan black belt, they begin to progress up the ladder toward tenth Dan, depending on how long they continue to study. Few students ever attain the rank of tenth Dan. This rank has traditionally been reserved for instructors who've had unique insights and talents that lead them to create their own system or style of martial art, like my teacher and mentor Ernie Lieb. For students to arrive at a level between sixth Dan and ninth Dan is a great accomplishment if their system places the emphasis on requirements deemed proper for such ranks. Sadly, in the US, there are many martial artists whose only goal is rank. Many don't really earn what they eventually claim. They either work under another instructor who they pay to receive a higher rank, or they start their own martial arts organization so they can promote themselves and like-minded friends. This pretentious mode of self-promotion has resulted in martial artists in other parts of the world looking at Americans and American martial artists as a bunch of clowns who aren't serious students of the arts.

When I returned from Spain to the United States in October of 1970, I had just earned my second degree black belt. I continued to follow the tournament scene via *Black Belt* magazine while stationed overseas. I was anxious to try my hand as a black belt. Without beleaguering you with accounts of my many tournament stories, suffice it to say, I was able to pick up some forty-plus trophies over the years. For every trophy won, there were at least ten competitions where I got stomped; most of the time, it was by better competitors. However, there were times it was due to poor officiating and/or politics. I realize forty or so trophies are not a lot in comparison to many others who went to tournaments practically every weekend. My interests lie not so much in competition but in the desire to learn more about other aspects of the many systems that make up martial arts. Tournament competition was one part of my martial arts training that helped to build my confidence in different areas.

In high school, I never participated in sports to any degree. Not being a "jock" meant not being with the "in crowd" or wearing a letter jacket or sweater. There is a certain kind of self-confidence that results from winning in martial arts competition. I was no one really great, though I got mentioned once in *Black Belt* magazine by one of their correspondents as an "unknown newcomer." That was the result of my first black belt completion, after returning to the States from Spain. The tournament was held in Memphis, Tennessee, by Kang Rhee. I won the heavyweight division and placed third in the grand championship that night. I was also told by others that I had excellent potential to be one of the top-rated competitors in the nation. I did manage a rating as the top kata competitor in the American Karate System for the 1973–1974 time frame and the number two guy in the American Karate Association during the same time frame. There were times when I would leave a tournament with first place in kata and first, second, or third in heavyweight sparring. It was a good feeling to win knowing you'd done your best and were judged fairly among the many other good martial artists who competed.

Tournament competition is also a great way to find out how well your training has prepared you. You come up against many talented people when you compete. Unfortunately, there are just as many problems that occur at tournaments that cause competitors a great deal of heartbreak and frustration. If competition is kept in perspective and not made to be the panacea (cure-all) for all that the martial arts stands for, then the student has an excellent chance of seeing the big picture. It's this big picture from which enlightenment comes. It is as much from within us as it is from outside. Again, my interests lie not in seeing if I was the best fighter or kata competitor but in broadening my intellectual horizons in martial arts and my understanding of myself. It has also been in teaching others that have greatly helped me in developing myself personally.

Commercialism vs. Traditionalism

Over the past fifty-nine years, I've had the opportunity to visit and train in a number of schools across the nation and overseas. Some schools were purely commercial. The people who ran them made their living by getting as many paying students through their doors as possible. Other schools were located in YMCAs, churches, and community or recreation centers. These schools were more interested in teaching their style, so the students' perspective was more in line with the Asian way of thinking. One commercial school with which I developed an ongoing relationship is located in McAllen, Texas. The owner and head instructor, David Borowitz, works at instilling a proper mind-set in his students while still making a living from full-time instruction. He tries to not sacrifice the quality of the instruction or the importance of earning rank, like some of the other commercial schools in the area. I'm sure there are other such schools located throughout the US where their instructors do their best to meet and keep this same balance.

Overseas, the dojos were run more along the lines of clubs than commercial schools, though there were a number of them whose instructors also earned a living from full-time teaching. It didn't appear, from what I saw in Europe of the schools I visited or trained in, that they were as consumed by generating profits as many of their American counterparts. The key difference here is where one draws the line between quantity and quality. My experience has shown me that the biggest violators of quantity over quality are the Koreans. Let me also say I have known some really good Korean instructors whose main objective was turning out good students as well as generating funds. There are also a lot of good commercial schools with solid traditional values.

Commercialism has its place if approached properly. Students should not be produced in a McDojo assembly-line fashion from white to black belt as soon as they know the techniques and movements, purely for generating funds as quickly as possible. This does a great disservice to the students, as well as the martial arts community. Nearly everyone has heard a joke or story about the guy who, in the heat of an argument jumps, back into a karate stance while announcing he either knows karate or has a black belt. The other guy, totally unimpressed, responds, "Yeah, well, I know tire iron," and commences to put lumps on the other's head. When instructors who haven't received proper training and instruction run schools, the result is poorly taught students in the majority of cases. During a tournament in Edinburg, Texas, I was the center referee in a ring of advanced-level (under black belt) teens. During one match, the young man who won hit the other on two different occasions with no intention of using even the smallest amount of control. After warning him twice, I gave his opponent a point when he hit the other boy again with no control. Even though he won the match, his brother, a black belt with the same school, argued with me saying it didn't matter if the contact was too hard. A point was a point. I admonished him for his lack of respect and poor attitude. I was told later he was making faces at me behind my back. The instructor of these two youths was totally responsible for their lack of respect and sportsmanship. Even though I confronted him about it, I doubt seriously he cared. I was reminded of the movie *The Karate Kid* in which the instructor of the Kobu Kai School teaches his students to show no mercy. His students reflected his bad attitude and poor sportsmanship to the letter. I also have it on good authority this same instructor, now an eighth Dan, wasn't even a black belt twenty years prior. I earned my first Dan in May 1968 and my ninth Dan in June 2007. This last promotion was to be chief instructor of the American Karate System. This became necessary after the tragic and untimely death of our organization's founder and chief instructor, Ernest H. Lieb. Though this example speaks less of commercialism, it does illustrate (sadly) where some so-called students of martial arts heads really are. They are the kinds of martial artists the European's call clowns. For them, it's more about image, rank, and ego than anything else; as a result, these instructors turn out students who are their mirror image.

Commercialism also seems to promote a larger number of young students to the rank of black belt. Go to any of a variety of karate or Tae Kwon Do schools and you'll have no trouble finding boys and girls seven and eight years of age wearing a black belt. One of the key positions and philosophies we in the American Karate System have had since our inception has been to not promote kids to black belt. We feel they must be mature enough to understand the significance and importance of the black-belt rank. We set seventeen as the age at which some level of maturity should exist enough to understand and appreciate the significance of the rank they have achieved. That includes knowing how they should conduct themselves in a given situation, thus ensuring (as best one can) they won't abuse or misuse these skills. When abuse of skills takes place, it results in a poor misrepresentation of the arts and the student's true training. More recently this age limit was relaxed. Senior members of the AKS felt there were younger people who had worked hard and demonstrated the proper attitude and level of maturity required. It was decided to look at younger members on a case-by-case basis.

This is an area (outside of commercial influences) where more traditionally minded teachers can have a profound impact. The study and training of martial arts should emphasize the goal of developing the person into a more productive and responsible member of society, not just another number on a list of students who attained the rank of black belt about which the head instructor can brag. The main reason a qualified black belt begins to teach others is to pass on to them what he or she has learned. With proper training, the student's development is always along positive lines. Unfortunately, many people who get involved in martial arts haven't done well elsewhere in life. Consequently, people have found an area where they have been able to succeed to some extent. They use this as their avenue to gain the limelight. Anyone who has been to a few tournaments will know exactly what I mean. Martial arts is one area I've come across where a great number of egotists exist. As I've gotten older, I've come to realize the arena of politics is another. There is nothing wrong with having a somewhat inflated ego if it's kept in check and in perspective. When it's not, you have instructors and their assistants who provide the wrong example for their students. If a student scores a point on this type of person during a sparring session, he will likely beat the poor kid into the ground. His ego won't permit him to be seen as anything but invincible. If a pretty girl walks into the school, the egotist immediately begins to show his stuff. Girls are not exempt from this either. In their case, it may revolve more around chasing the instructor than trying to demonstrate invincibility.

So where does this put us in regard to commercial schools and noncommercial ones? It requires an approach that looks at what the motivating factors are for a black belt to open a school. It requires an understanding of this person's background and legitimacy as it pertains to how he or she got a black belt, along with the lineage of their instructor and his. What are their qualifications? How much time have they spent on their studies and training? To what degree and depth have they studied martial arts history and philosophy? These are some areas that can be used as a jumping-off point in developing a clear view of the individual's qualifications to teach others. One of the biggest problems in the United States today is the lack of organized control be it local, state, or federal, with the goal of establishing minimum standards for the licensing instructors. This would be a crucial step toward providing a means of verification that an instructor possesses the minimum requirements and qualifications necessary to teach. Without this control, it's a wide-open ballgame in which anyone can play. There are no rules or guidelines to govern who does what to whom. The result is a lot of misled and cheated students who sought instruction, only to be taken to the cleaners by a smart con man, or those students who received instructions from someone completely lacking the qualifications. There are hundreds of quality schools and teachers throughout the US today. A person wishing to learn a particular style or art needs only to take the time to visit a variety of them and observe how their classes are run. By observing their classes and asking pointed and well-structured questions, a person will soon see what the instructor's goals are. Also, talking with some of the students will help in shedding additional light on what makes this school successful.

Thoughts and Commentary

I've been a part of the American Karate System (AKS) since 1972 and a student of the arts in general since February of 1960. I liked what Mr. Lieb was doing then, as I do now. We're not constrained by traditional guidelines for the most part, though we conduct ourselves as traditionalists in many ways. While other schools might not entertain change, the AKS looks to improve wherever possible. There are a few areas where we too need to evaluate our techniques and direction. I used to believe these areas would be taken care of, not hidden or swept under the carpet, as some systems do to keep from disturbing so-called traditionalistic values. An example of failure in this area was a restructuring of the sequence of our katas (forms) to put them more in line with their respective progression of difficulty. Before Mr. Lieb died, he and I had discussed this. He understood the rationale and was on board. Later on, discussions with another senior member, now my replacement as chief instructor, Fred Reinecke, resulted in his understanding and agreement for the change. With one single exception, those members with whom I discussed this change were on board. The end result was one person kept the organization from improving and moving forward because they didn't want to support me in meaningful change.

Our system is the first truly American one to date. Now you ask, "How can there be an American system of karate?" A system or style of martial art does not have to originate from an Oriental country. Over the centuries, many ways of fighting and defense, with and without weapons, have come and gone, but many are still with us today. If a person studies the histories of the many prominent styles of karate today, he will find many of these styles came into being during the last century. So why shouldn't there be an American style of karate? The AKS uses the main Oriental systems and philosophies as its foundational cornerstones. This includes six of our under black belt katas, which are taken from three of the main countries where various styles evolved. Like these other countries, America has had its forms of fighting and has evolved over the years. This evolution has been the result of Americans learning other fighting arts while living in the orient. In addition, Americans have learned from Orientals who have come to our country with their arts to teach us.

The AKS requires its students and instructors to conform to rigid requirements in training, testing, and attitude, both in and out of the school environment. This parallels other oriental systems in many respects and surpasses them in others. Our black belts must physically test through sixth Dan. Most other styles only test through fourth or fifth Dan levels. I could go on with additional rationale and justifications about why the AKS is so good, as well as being a legitimate style. This is not to say, as some are fond of doing, that my system is the best. No one style is any worse or better than any other. The individual who represents his respective art is the one who either does a good or bad job of portraying what his system can or cannot do.

When I became a student of Mr. Lieb and the AKS, I was working on my third Dan with a Korean instructor. I'd learned one set of forms for my first Dan and a second set for my second Dan. When I got back to the States, I was told I would have to learn another new set of katas before I could test for third Dan. It gave me the impression the Koreans were having trouble deciding on what to do and which forms were best. You would have thought after centuries of martial history they would have gotten a handle on that already. I'd been in the Korean system some ten years, yet I never felt like anything more than just a student. While a student under some of my Korean instructors, there were times I was the one teaching the classes. There were also times where I felt there was a great deal of respect missing, not to mention the impression of being more of a dollar sign than a black belt assistant instructor. I don't mean this to sound bitter, but I expected more from the senior instructor than just instruction. As in any organization, loyalty, friendship, and trust must be earned and given in both directions.

For me, the study of karate was more than just learning how to kick and punch. It was becoming part of something that has a rich history, even though many cultures are involved. The self-discipline and desire to acquire the capabilities and knowledge demonstrated by Orientals are to be admired. The true study of the arts means accepting it as a way of life. American students tend to be lazy, afraid of a little work, and impatient for results. It's good to ask questions in order to improve one's understanding. It's also important to follow instructions without questioning them as well. A student must trust his teacher to provide him in his learning environment with both physical and intellectual instruction. Obviously, his teacher must be qualified enough to provide the appropriate level and depth of instruction based on the level and ability of the student. The student must also know when to ask questions and when to pay attention and work. American students also give up too easily or become bored and want to move on to something else. If things start to get difficult, quitting seems to be the easiest way out. In fairness to Americans, I was told by a Shotokan friend of mine, Ariel Lim, when he started training in the Philippines at the university, there were five hundred students. When he tested for his black belt five years later, there were only seven. The point is not everyone is cut out for martial arts training and its lifestyle. Those who become successful in martial arts have a much higher likelihood of being successful in life as well.

Recommendations

If you are a student of martial arts, or desire to become one, examine your reason and resolve. Search your mind and your heart for the true reason and don't start with any misgivings. Know that your studies will take years. Understand the key to success requires patience and perseverance. Though the end results tend to be a long way down the road, they are well worth working for. I have come to the point where I am comfortable with who I am and what my abilities and inabilities are. I have no illusions of being anything more than I am. I seek no higher goals than continuing to be one with my environment and my society. My joy is in seeing the light in the eyes of a student with whom I have just shown or explained something that they eventually grasped. I have nothing to prove to anyone save myself, for it is only my God and myself I must please and serve. By helping students understand movements and/or principles, I have earned rewards for which there is no monetary equivalence. Being there for someone who is having problems for which they feel no escape also provides fulfillment. What each person must do in his or her own mind is to plot a path and travel it. We are the planters of our own seeds and must stand ready to reap the results, be they good or bad.

In Gichin Funakoshi's autobiography, *Karate-Do, My Way of Life*, he writes,

> *A Japanese actively seeking self-enlightenment will say that he is "training his stomach" (hara wo neru). Although the expression has wide implications, its origin lies in the obvious necessity to*

harden the muscles of the stomach, a prerequisite for
the practice of karate, which is, after all, a com-
bat technique. By bringing the stomach muscles to a
state of perfection, a karateka is able to control not
only the movements of his hands and feet but also his
breathing. (P. viii)

The practice of karate, or any martial art, requires dedication. The dual meaning behind Funakoshi's discussion of *hara wo neru* was first the literal meaning of the toughening of the stomach. The second more philosophical one was to train and develop our minds and bodies. By approaching our training from the latter, we then seek to arrive at a point of self-enlightenment. To some, that would be the point where we become totally comfortable with who we are and what our capabilities and inabilities are.

Also, the study of martial arts requires courtesy, respect, and sincerity be given and received by all. This is also a good point Sensei Egami made in his book. He said,

He who could follow the way of karate must
be courteous, not only in training but in daily life.
While humble and gentle, he should never be servile.
His performance of the kata should reflect boldness
and confidence. This seemingly paradoxical combi-
nation of boldness and gentleness leads ultimately
to harmony. It is true, as Master Funakoshi used to
say, that the spirit of karate would be lost without
courtesy. (p. 18)

The one movement that best reflects this attitude is taught the very first day a person begins his or her studies. It encompasses respect, courtesy, humility, and sincerity. Yet people are concerned they aren't doing it right. You're wondering what movement could embody so much. It is the simple bow. Sensei Egami puts it very nicely. *"Without sincerity, the bow is meaningless. Rather than be con-cerned about its outward appearance, put your heart and soul into the bow, then it will naturally take on a good shape"* (p. 18). As with all things one endeavors to accomplish in life, the results are always better when we have put our hearts and souls into the effort, with sincerity, courtesy, and respect. The efforts merit the results.

Memoriam

On September 22, 2006, my dear friend, teacher, and mentor of more than thirty-three years was tragically killed in Lathen, Germany. Ernie was traveling with Chuck Krum a retired US Army senior NCO, affectionately known to all as Sergeant Pepper, and two of our German members. They were riding on an experimental train that struck a maintenance car. Along with our members, there were twenty-one others who died.

Over the past decade, Ernie had discussed with me and several of the other senior black belts his desires for leadership and control of the AKS in the event he was no longer with us. All of us figured this wouldn't be anything we'd really need to concern ourselves with. Ernie was getting more into the development and building of the AKS as time went along. His yearly trips to Germany to conduct seminars, coupled with his efforts at home, had helped to focus his energies. He saw a bright future for the AKS and was enthusiastic. I remember jokingly telling him he would probably outlive most of us.

Part of Ernie's concerns was the survival of his beloved organization. The examples left by what had happened to Ed Parker's International Kempo Karate organization and Robert Trias's United States Karate Association after their deaths remained ever present in Ernie's mind. The organizations those two pioneers of American karate built fell into disunity after their respective deaths because of petty squabbles and large egos among the senior black belts. The senior students of these two great men could not come together regarding who the leader of their respective organizations should be. The end result was both organizations became fragmented and broke into smaller groups. The legacies of these two great pioneers were lost in the dust of the power struggles that ensued following their passing.

To Mr. Lieb's credit, he had already taken steps to let his senior black belts know who he wanted to take over as the chief instructor in the event of his death. After his funeral on October 4, 2006, I was named his successor. During our first summer camp, without our beloved leader and friend, my succession was formalized with my promotion to ninth Dan. Since then, I've had offers by others from other organizations to be promoted to tenth-degree black belt. I've respectfully declined them all. Out of respect for Mr. Lieb, I, like other senior AKS black belts, will not accept a rank that would put me on the same level as him. Most martial artists understand this level of loyalty and respect it.

In reflecting back over the years I've been training and studying the martial arts, I never once imagined ever arriving at the rank I now hold or being responsible for the leadership of an international organization. I also never expected to be inducted into the Master's Hall of Fame either. Thankfully, I was initially surrounded by senior black belts who shared the same vision and goals. During the black belt meeting, it became clear those present were unanimous in their desire to see the dream and legacy of our founder continued. They voiced their collective trust in our two assistant chief instructors (Fred Reinecke and Dave Thomas) and in your humble correspondent.

The tragic and sudden loss of our founder and friend left a large void in our hearts and the training halls that make up the American Karate System. What remains is what he instilled in all of us who were privileged to train under him. Many of us were all honored by his enduring friendship. He taught us the importance of treating all students with kindness, humility, and patience. He taught us to be competitive but always good sportsmen. He emphasized the need to learn from other styles while sharing. Most importantly, he taught us that the person who represents their respective styles either does it honor or shame, inferring that all styles have both good and bad aspects. The challenge is to adopt the good and leave the bad behind if it can't be improved on.

Conclusion

In December of 2016, I was diagnosed with bladder cancer. I was already dealing with stressful situations within the AKS, referred to by most as just politics. Politics is one thing; childish petty immaturity—something else altogether. One of our senior members has been holding a grudge against another senior member for several decades. The alleged reason: because of bad treatment he felt the latter had done to some of his students. Whether that was true or not, no one really knows. What I witnessed was someone saying something the other person took the wrong way. Even if it was true, it should have been put in the past. Constantly hating someone and never forgiving is unhealthy and pathological. This has been an ongoing problem for many years. Before I became the chief instructor, I didn't have to deal with it. Afterward, it became a frustration.

In the summer of 2016, during the annual summer camp, I was made aware that I had allegedly said something that had offended this same individual's wife. This allegedly took place during the summer camp of 2012. So for four years, this guy has held a grudge against me. A person I felt was a close and dear friend. True friends will tell you if you've said or done something that has offended them or a loved one. They don't treat you coldly and talk about you behind your back like middle school adolescent children. My student Dr. Michael Coyle and I were late when we arrived at his house for dinner. This is when I allegedly made the insulting statement. We were also accused of being drunk. I had never seen this level of lying and complete deceit on this man's part. He demonstrated a clear lack of honor and integrity. This put a great deal more clarity and understanding on why he had continuously (for years) talked badly about the other senior black belt. What's even sadder is this man and woman professed to be Christians. Clearly, their inability to forgive demonstrated how little they understood what being a Christian really means. While I was deeply hurt, I have forgiven them for the lies and deceit that took place.

This is the certificate presented to me in August at the 2008 Master's Hall of Fame awards and Induction Ceremonies in Anaheim, California

I initially told a couple of people I would be retiring officially at the next summer camp. July of 2017, I stepped down and turned things over to Mr. Reinecke. The cancer was dealt with in February of 2017 with a surgery that lasted over seven and a half hours. I have still have been dealing with kidney issues, but the main worry has been taken care of. The weight off my shoulders in knowing I would no longer have to listen to the childish bickering and lies on the part of some AKS members, coupled with knowing cancer had been taken care of, was great. No longer would I have to listen to people wanting to grow the organization but not willing to do the work necessary to make that happen. The list goes on.

I served as the leader and chief instructor of the AKS from the summer of 2007, after the passing of Mr. Lieb, until I retired at the summer camp of 2017. Over the years, I'd learned most of the members saw the organization and their participation as nothing more than a hobby. When we held regional training camps in either West Virginia or Ohio, many didn't bother to attend. They had sports or family events which were more important to attend. The fact that the dates for these training weekends were known months ahead of time made little difference. The more engaged members, those who wanted to see the organization grow, made every effort to attend and participate. This was a frustration they often verbalized as well. I was learning more and more about the frustration Ernie had dealt with for so many years.

There were other things I tried to do that had the support of the majority of the others, which were also shot down by the same person mainly because of his angst with me. This petty mentality kept the organization from changing the kata sequences, kept the organization from working toward becoming a 501 © 3 nonprofit organization, along with requiring black belts to take on more responsibility within the AKS. The goal of becoming a nonprofit was to provide money for those who wanted to train but couldn't afford uniforms and other equipment. People who wanted to attend training seminars or the summer camp but didn't have the money for travel expenses. The utter lack of vision on the part of one person has and will continue to keep the AKS from growing and making improvements

The two main areas I was able to make happen was building an AKS website and getting the organization on the Internet (April of 1999). I also worked with my student JD Hunt in developing a student handbook (initial printing in 1992) so each member club or school had the same basic requirements, thus unifying the AKS under the same set of standard requirements was done with little to no help from any of them. We compiled handouts and information used by the different AKS schools and clubs into a single student handbook. Over the years, Ernie pushed to get everyone on board. Every school has complied save one. To this day, this school still makes excuses for not issuing new student handbooks to the beginners. They prefer instead to continue using one their head instructor had put together some years previously.

Sadly, I'm afraid the AKS is on a downhill slide toward oblivion. As a result, this organization I gave much of my life to (forty-six years) will eventually cease to exist. The fault will lie with those members who hold petty grudges and lack any vision for the future. It didn't take long after Mr. Lieb's passing for me to realize why he'd chosen me to succeed him. Little did he know how things would turn out after his death.

The ideas expressed in this paper can best be summed up by the following creed:

American Karate System
Mission Statement

The goals and mission of the American Karate System continue the dream and legacy of its founder Ernest H. Lieb. It is our pledge to accomplish this by adhering to the following:

1. Strive for excellence in training and the conduct of your personal life.
2. Foster the technical, mental, and personal development of AKS members.
3. Maintain traditional ideologies while approaching training from an eclectic point of view.
4. Teach effective techniques, tactics, and strategies for self-defense and/or defense of the helpless, while educating the public about the true nature of the martial arts.
5. Represent the AKS with dignity, honor, and integrity at all times.
6. Espouse the noble virtues of humility and honor in training and social interaction whether in public or in private.
7. Participate in competition with sportsmanship.

8. Promote open engagement and mutual sharing of martial art training experiences with members of other styles and organizations.

As members of the American Karate System, we should all strive to be the best we can while helping each other. What we do must not be based on greed or any desire for self-gratification beyond our own improvement and that of our fellow members. There is no place for petty immature attitudes or childish grudges. These things only serve to destroy what Mr. Lieb and those of us who joined with him in 1973 chose to develop and grow as an American style of Karate.

A portrait also used on the web site

Bibliography

The Way of Karate, Beyond Technique, by Shigeru Egami, Kodansha International Ltd., 1st Edition, 1976

Karate-Do, My Way of Life, by Gichin Funakoshi, Kodansha International Ltd., 1st Edition, 1975

Karate-Do Nuju Kajo To Sono Kai-Setsu, by Gichin Funakoshi, Karate-Do Taikan. 1938 Edition, G

Back to the Military

Now that I've injected the martial arts background, the reader should have a better idea as to the types of training and studies I engaged in and their effects on me in my life.

In February of 1977, I reported to Lackland AFB and the USAF Security Police Academy. Janie remained in the Valley working and taking care of our daughter Erica. It was difficult for me to walk around Lackland, a basic training base where the USAF Security Police Academy is located, because everywhere I went, there were young airman and women saluting and holding doors for me. It wasn't all that long ago I'd been doing that for the officers at Sheppard and Moron. It brought me to the understanding I had entered a new chapter in my life that now included new responsibilities. It required me to understand I now was assuming a leadership role.

When I graduated at the end of April of that year, I picked Janie and Erica up and we relocated to Tinker AFB in Oklahoma City. I was to be the first officer in charge of security for the new E3-A AWAC aircraft being based there. I had a senior noncommissioned officer (NCO) named Jim Disney, who taught me a lot about being an officer and supervising my enlisted troops. When we'd first met, I told him while I had the rank, he had the knowledge. I was looking to him to teach me and keep me from doing anything stupid. He was a good teacher.

While at Tinker AFB, I was sent on a temporary duty (TDY) assignment to Saudi Arabia. The Saudis were purchasing two different types of fighter jets from the USA. I and a lieutenant colonel joined twenty-one engineers in Riyadh, Saudi Arabia. For thirty days, we spent time on several of their air bases. The engineers were looking at what new infrastructure would be needed to support the new aircraft the Saudis were buying. I was tasked with looking at the physical security of several of these bases and their visitor control.

At some locations, the rock outcropping was so bad you had to drill and dynamite the boulders in order to try and set up sensors. You could use buried sensors that left some type of microwave capability or fence disturbance alarms. Even then the Bedouins herders would cut the fence so their flocks could pass through. None of the Saudi security people said anything because of the Bedouins' right to go where they pleased in the country. The month I spent there was more of a culture shock than any other part of the world I'd ever been in.

When I first arrived in Saudi Arabia, landing in Jeddah, I walked out of the terminal to look at the city. If there hadn't been any cars or electric poles lining the streets, I would have sworn I was back in the tenth century. This was my first up-close encounter with Muslims and the Middle East. Their culture and restrictions on women were completely contrary to everything I'd been taught in my life to that point. Later in my career, while working on my master's degree, I would learn more about the Middle East, along with her people, culture, and religion.

Shortly after returning to Oklahoma that spring of 1978, I was sent as part of a pilot group of sixteen security police officers to undergo the Infantry Officers Basic Course (IOBC) and learn small unit tactics from the Army Rangers in Georgia at Fort Benning. While the training was difficult at times, it was very fulfilling. I found training like that took me out of my comfort zone and made me face things I would not have ordinarily had to deal with.

The result was a whole new group of skill sets and an elevated level of self-confidence. A lot of media personalities try to talk like they know what military training is like. If you have never undergone it you're clueless. There is absolutely no replacing the strain and pain that comes with exertion and giving it everything you've got for several weeks or months. They made you dig down deep and hit it hard virtually every day.

No, the vast majority of media types and liberals, in general, have no clue. Nor do they have the backbone and patriotic spirit it takes to go through the rigors this kind of training entails. The only way that could possibly happen would be if we still had the draft. Even then, many of these people would desert north to Canada where they could hide in order to avoid being drafted. No different than during the Vietnam era draft. These people are great at talking and demonstrating but utterly lacking in the backbone it takes to wear the uniform of our country and fight to preserve what it stands for. They love the lifestyle and freedom but don't want to do what it takes to protect and preserve it.

Learning to survive in the woods on little to no sleep, how to camouflage yourself so people walk right by you without knowing you're there, moving quietly in all kinds of weather and terrain, and getting by on one meal a day was only part of what we learned. We also learned military tactics and strategy, coupled with the leadership skills needed to maneuver men in combat. We learned a leader must lead by example, from the front. This is something not everyone is cut out for. And of course, we became experts with a variety of different weapons and weapon systems.

One of the key reasons this pilot group was created and sent to Benning was to develop more infantry-trained security police (SP) officers who could help in establishing and growing the Air Base Ground Defense program for the USAF. This newly developed and growing program within the USAF Security Forces dealt with defending our air bases in theaters of war or conflict. While it was the US Army Military Police, under their area security mission, who was tasked with that protection, the reality was they were to spread out and not manned or equipped sufficiently for the challenge. It was up to the USAF Sky-Cops to undertake and handle that mission.

This would entail setting up listening and observations posts. Determining where the likely avenues of approach were so we could target them with our 81 mm mortars. We had to be able to send out regular patrols with the capability of neutralizing the enemy before they could get within standoff weapons range, which would allow them to damage the airfield and affect our air missions.

After the training at Fort Benning, I returned home a slim 178 pounds. Not bad since I was pushing the scales at 205 before I left for Georgia nearly five months earlier. Without question, I was in the best shape of my life. Things back at Tinker were clicking along, and I was soon back in the swing of my old routine. Part of that was my position as the Tactical Neutralization Team (TNT) leader, just another term for a SWAT (Special Weapons and Tactics) team.

One day, I went to check up on my TNT troops. They were practicing rappelling from a four-story high fire tower. When I got out there, it never dawned on me I'd be climbing that tower to do the same. This is significant because I've always been a proponent of leading by example. It's also significant because I'm *very* afraid of heights.

That being said, though, I climbed the ladder to the top strapped on the swiss seat (the webbing they use to connect the rope too that wraps around your waist and both legs), hooked the rope to the D ring (the metal connecter attached to the swiss seat), and positioned myself on the edge of the building. *Holy cow! Am I really doing this?* Needless to say, my heart was in my throat. I started releasing rope as I leaned backward. Nothing happened. I stood up and released a little more rope then began leaning backward again. Still nothing happened. I repeated this process again. As I was leaning backward, all of a sudden, my feet slid down the side of the building until the rope became tight. There is no doubt in my mind my heart had stopped for at least four to five beats. wow, what an experience.

I went back up four more times to repeat the rappelling experience down the side of the building. I found I was able to meet and overcome my fear. Clearly, the only way to increase you confidence and skill sets as you go through life is to force yourself outside of your comfort zone and tackle them head-on. Part of being able to do that is putting your faith in God.

In the spring of 1979, I got orders for Germany. I was excited because Janie and I love traveling and learning about new places. We were stationed at Hessisch-Oldendorf in the state of Niedersachsen, northcentral Germany, affectionately called the "HOG." The air station was a support base for mobile air traffic control (ATC) units located several miles in two different directions.

Both Bad Münder and Schwelentrop were able to deploy portable ATC units to various locations in Northern Germany in order to provide ATC guidance to different types of antiarmor aircraft in the northern part of Germany by the Danish border. In Southern Germany, these actions were handled by well-established NATO air bases, which included several US ones. This was my first chief of security police job. It gave me great opportunities to get to know the local German population, as well as the British military since we were based in their sector.

Here, like in Spain, I started teaching karate on the German economy. One day (Saturday mornings) in the town of Hessisch-Oldendorf at the school gym, and another in a town (Rehren) just to the west of the air station some eight or so kilometers away in their school gym. I also took a German 101 class in order to learn how to properly pronounce their words, along with understanding the grammar. Little by little, I began learning my third language.

While stationed at Hessisch-Oldendorf, the American air base of Ramstein Air Base was bombed in August of 1981. A group called the Red Army Faction, a spin-off of the infamous Baader-Meinhof terrorist group, claimed responsibility for the act. Twelve US military personnel and two Germans were killed. Since a Muslim terrorist group had kidnapped and killed a number of Israeli athletes during the 1972 Munich Olympics, terrorist acts were on the rise. These attacks were mainly in Europe but later began raising their ugly heads in the Middle East. I was entering a new chapter of my life. I was learning more about the ugliness of terrorism and the hate leftist liberals in Europe and the Middle East have for Americans.

Terrorism was something many of us growing up in the '60s were familiar with. The Weather Underground, a radical communist group of university students, led by its self-appointed leader Bill Ayers, had bombed government buildings and robbed banks. Several members of their group were killed in an explosion that took place in one of their bomb-making factories. Ayers and his girlfriend Bernadine Dorhn never spent any real time in prison for their actions. Instead, they both earned degrees and are college professors in the Windy City, Chicago and good friends with Chicago's own Barack Hussein Obama.

The Symbionese Liberation Army was another domestic terror group who also robbed banks and had kidnapped the daughter (Patti) of newspaper publisher Randolph Hearst in February of 1974. They died in a shootout with California police. Patti survived and was prosecuted for her part in the group's criminal and terroristic activities. She was captured on video armed and participating in a bank robbery.

There was also another domestic terror group located in Puerto Rico. This group was known as Fuerzas Armadas de Liberacion Nacional Puertorriqueñia (Armed Force for National Liberation of Puerto Rico). They also bombed federal building and robbed banks. Some of them were captured, convicted, and sent to federal prison. Like the first two groups, this one was also a Marxist-Leninist terrorist group. No, terrorism was not really something new. In August of 1999, then President Bill Clinton offered clemency to sixteen members of the group if they renounced violence.

Barbra Olson wrote about this in her book *Final Days*. In her book, she writes about the excesses of Slick Willy's final days in office. Key among them were the pardons and clemencies he handed out. It seems his brother and Hillary were out beating the bushes looking for people who would be willing to buy them. To learn more, you should read her book. Sadly, on September 11, 2001, Mrs. Olson was on the hijacked flight that crashed in a field in Pennsylvania.

During a training exercise at Rhein-Main Air Base just outside of Frankfurt, Germany, while conducting patrolling tactics, my team came across a fire extinguisher bomb that was intended to blow up a set of railroad track junctions that would have derailed a train. Fortunately, the device was disarmed and rendered safe. The German police brought several busloads of cadets, and we all searched the surrounding woods and forest area for any other devices or signs that may have been left behind by the terrorists. We didn't find any more explosives, but we did uncover a cache of weapons that had been buried there. In the 1985 time frame, Rhein-Main experienced a similar bombing like Ramstein in 1981.

Terrorism against US entities took place in Europe during the 1980s, in addition to the two airbase bombing. The Army, Air Force Exchange Service (AFFES) in Frankfurt was bombed. Even though security and counterterrorism specialist told the brass to fence off the facility and place MPs to conduct 100 percent ID checks, they didn't take action until after the facility was bombed. Most of us commented about the lack of importance the brass gave those of us who were seen as subject matter experts (SMEs) until after what we'd predicted had taken place. This was not the only example where military bigwigs ignored the suggestions of the experts, only to end up spending several times more than they would have had to had they listened and acted when they had been warned.

It was during this exercise at Rhein-Main AB I met representatives from the Military Airlift Command (MAC) located at Scott AFB in Illinois. After several meetings and additional exercise involvement, I was invited to join the security police staff as the Air Base Ground Defense (ABGD) project officer. The plan was for that position to be my follow on assignment once I left Germany and returned to the States in June of 1982. Sadly, after finding out my mother had stage 4 lymphocytic lymphoma, I was rotated back to the States six months earlier in December of 1981.

Prior to returning to the United States, I promoted my student and fellow airman Robert Debelak to his first-degree black belt. Rob had been assigned to Hessisch-Oldendorf in 1980 and started training with me. He was a brown belt in a different style. Rob continued teaching the club I'd started and ended up marrying one of the German young ladies in the class. He and I would remain close and in contact with each other to this day.

During my tour of duty at Scott AFB, I was on the Military Airlift Command (MAC) for twelve months in the ABGD staff officer position. Being stationed at a major command like the Military Airlift gave me a new view and understanding of politics in the military. Full colonels would run errands for general officers. When the general barked, the colonel would jump. At smaller bases, these same colonels were the ones barking, which resulted in lesser-ranked officers jumping. Don't ever let someone tell you there's no politics in the military. Once you get promoted to lieutenant colonel or master sergeant, the rest of the way up depends all too often on whom you know.

I was moved from the MAC staff to the base level SP unit to fill in as the operations officer (like an assistant chief position) for the base security police. Once a replacement was found, I again moved to the Air Force Communications Command (AFCC) as the security police operations (ops) officer for the AFCC. While working as the major commands SP ops officer, I traveled to Okinawa, Korea, and the Philippines either as an augmenter to the inspector general's staff or as an inspector reviewing the security of remotely located communications facilities. Here again, I was able to see how other people of different cultures made a living or just barely managed to exist.

I was in this position until receiving orders in the summer of 1984 to redeploy to RAF Upper Heyford in the United Kingdom. Here, I was assigned to the Twentieth Security Police Squadron as its operations officer (equivalent to a civilian assistant police chief). This was by far the biggest and toughest job I'd had during my time as an officer in the USAF security police.

Heyford was an air base just outside Oxford, a few miles west of London, with a nuclear mission. There were two distinct areas on the base that required a security force of 450 personnel (airman). This was due to the various positions requiring security personnel over a 24/7 time frame. One area had aircraft on alert. These aircrafts were required to be airborne within five minutes of the alarm going off. Each of these F-111s carried tactical nuclear bombs. The second area was the weapons storage area where there were a number of bunkers full of conventional and tactical nuclear bombs. To accomplish this security mission, I had 5 officers and 450 enlisted personnel assigned to me.

There was an additional eighty enlisted personnel assigned to me strictly for law enforcement purposes. These guys and gals worked closely with the British Ministry of Defense (MOD) police. Since the American military was not supposed to lay hands on a British citizen, the MOD police were assigned to work with us in the event a disturbance involved one of their citizens.

Normal days at Heyford were about ten hours. There were many others that went from twelve to eighteen, depending on if we were being inspected by one of the many government organizations that oversaw the various missions the base was involved in. There were other times when we were in exercise mode that also resulted in long hours on the job.

During the August and September time frame of 1985, I was sent to Royal Air Force (RAF) Bentwaters/Woodbridge, just north of Ipswich, to be part of a planning group. Our responsibility was to develop and write the plans for war games involving the USA's part in the United Kingdom's (UK) first Homeland defense exercise since World War II. After completing the plans for US force involvement, I and another captain with the Office of Special Investigation were sent to the United Kingdom Land Forces (UKLF) headquarters in Salisbury in the south of England. Our job during the weeklong exercise was to follow the US participation and provide daily briefings to the British general staff at the UKLF HQ.

Me demonstrating a kicking technique
to one of my German Students

In the fall of 1985, I was given orders to report to Lindsey Air Station in Wiesbaden, Germany. At Lindsey, I became part of a newly formed unit that was charged with collocated operating base (COB) support. While we had a number of US air bases in Europe, there weren't enough to handle all the air assets that would deploy there in the event the Warsaw Pact countries of the United Soviet Socialist Republic (USSR) attacked. It was, therefore, necessary to work with six of our NATO allies (the Germans, Belgium, the Netherlands, Denmark, the Canadians, and the British). Among this group, there were twenty-five NATO bases in and around these respective Western European countries. Our job was to travel to these bases, meet with our counterparts and build plans for going to war, and for participating in exercises.

From the fall of 1985 until my family and I returned to the USA in June of 1988, our unit traveled around Western Europe, working with these allies, developing plans that would go into effect in the USSR attacked.

For my part and my young enlisted staff sergeant Jeff Fields, we were to focus on how the stateside deploying units would assimilate with their respective host and take responsibility for the security and defense of their assigned part of the base. At each location, Jeff and I worked closely with our counterparts to ensure we had the best possible understanding of the base's customs and operational requirements. That facilitated in writing the plans in a manner the deploying units could easily understand. Jeff was an invaluable asset. He was a hard worker and a quick study. His efforts and knowledge made my job very easy.

It was while stationed at Lindsey Air Station I began working on my master's degree in international relations. The degree was offered by Troy State University, whose main campus was located in Alabama. The focus of my studies was the Middle East. It was clear to many of us that understanding this area of the world, its people, religion, and customs would be invaluable as the problem grew.

Terrorism was on the rise. Middle Eastern terrorists were becoming known as Jihadists who were more than willing to sacrifice themselves (shahids) for their beliefs and faith in Islam (martyrdom).

As I continued my studies, I also wrote papers on subjects that dealt with terrorism. By understanding what drove these people to commit suicide in the name of their religion, I was able to see how utterly fanatical and dangerous they were. We have similar types in America on the religious right. People who translate the Bible to meet their bigot ideologies. While not as violent as Middle Eastern zealots, they were filled with just as much hate.

After completing my tour of duty in Germany in June of 1988, I was assigned to Fort McClellan in Anniston, Alabama. I was assuming duties as the Air Force exchange officer to the US Army Military Police (MP) School and headquarters. In the words of my fellow Army colleagues, I was their token "wingnut." Anyone who has served in the military knows full well the interservice rivalries that exist. Each service loves to poke fun at the others. Yet when the chips are down, you will not find a tighter group of people who will be there for each other. This is one of the big differences between conservatives and liberals. The liberal is in it for him- or herself. They collaborate with others as long as it suits them. Here again, all one has to do is watch politicians. When doing so, always remember to listen to what they say but pay closer attention to what they do. They tell you what they want you to believe while their actions show you their true intentions.

During my two years at Fort McClellan, I learned more about the US Army's MP missions and how they fit into the air-land battle doctrine. I worked in the directorate of combat development. I was bringing the Air Force's views and perspectives. One of the frustrations I had with my air force colleagues was their Union card mentality. It didn't make any difference whether they turned wrenches, pushed papers, worked on aircraft or served food. Their view about combat was that it was our (the SPs) job to protect the base and its personnel. They couldn't understand the simple fact that the enemy doesn't differentiate between combat and noncombat personnel. If you wore a uniform, you were an enemy soldier and would be treated accordingly.

After completing my assignment at Fort McClellan, I was stationed at Chanute AFB in Rantoul, Illinois, in June of 1990. I was the last commander and chief of security police at the base. We began downsizing in preparation for closing the base in 1993. Chanute was part of the Air Training Command (ATC) and provided various technical schools for different aircraft-support jobs and firefighters. I was still involved in singing during church services. Returning to the Air Force and the base chapel reinvigorated that activity. I was also privileged to work with the Air Force Band of the West as a guest vocalist.

Shortly after arriving at Chanute AFB, Operation Desert Storm began. My security police squadron sent out supplies and personnel to support the efforts in Kuwait. With a reduced number of SPs, we were forced to change our base patrol zones from five to two, and to close two of the three gates on the base perimeter used by military and civilian personnel to come and go. One of the gates was by the enlisted housing area. Its closure caused the installation commander, a one-star general, to receive letters from very unhappy residents living in base housing. After a meeting with the general, my boss, the base commander, and the commanders of several of the training groups, we created a security police augmentee program. This program allowed us to use personnel selected from other organization for training up to a three level as an SP in order for them to man the gates, thus freeing up career Sky-Cops to patrol and perform other appropriate police duties.

As we were coming into the fall of 1992, it was apparent that George H. W. Bush was not going to win reelection. Thanks to Ross Perot, who took enough of the conservative vote to give the election to Clinton, Bush was a one-term president. As I'd mentioned earlier, those of us on active duty began to learn about Clinton's dislike for the military as the campaign season wore on. I turned forty-five that October (1992) and was about to hit the twenty-year mark of my Air Force career. I made the choice to retire and put in my papers two months before my lieutenant colonel's board met. Clinton won the election. It was time to go. My wife was not happy with my decision. While she loved being part of the military, she respected my decision and helped me close that chapter of our lives. In hindsight, it turned out to be the right decision.

Once the Democrats had control of the government, and by extension the military, the "political correctness" bug began infecting both military life and the way it conducted its business. From that point forward, the military ceased to be the same. A person had to be careful about what they said. If another person mistook or misconceived a comment or joke, a person's career could be ended. This was also around the time of the Navy's Tailhook incident in Las Vegas and the Supreme Court nomination process of Clarence Thomas. The military became so afraid of its own shadow, any female accusation against a male resulted in the male being on the losing end. That usually meant some level of disciplinary action, but typically a letter of reprimand. The result of this was the end of the individual's career. If he had a line number for promotion that too was gone.

As a military veteran, I'm am saddened and very disappointed that we have a group of people in this country (liberals) who disdain and even hate what the military stands for, let alone what it does to keep our people free and safe. Observations of Democrats' mishandling and abuse of the military (e.g., Clinton's use of the military in Bosnia or the bombing of an aspirin factory in Africa to distract from his sex scandals at home) coupled with their failure to support them when they most needed it (e.g., Mogadishu and Benghazi) are convincing examples of their complete incompetence as leaders. Because of the animosity they hold toward the military and civilian versions of it in our law enforcement communities, they have no respect for the men and women who serve.

These are people who put their lives on the line daily so American citizens may go about their business and live their lives in peace and safety. Add to this politicians who were either forced into the military by their parents because it would be good for their political aspirations (Al Gore) or those who joined for the same reason (John Kerry). These are people who don't deserve the respect or the authority they received by being elected to political offices. Fortunately, neither of these guys won their party's election for the presidency. For me, they are examples of the problem with our political system and the narcissistic arrogance of the people who run for office.

Major M. A. Sullenger a couple of years
before his retirement in June of 1993

Retiring from the Military

After finalizing my retirement paperwork at Chanute, I joined my family in Raymondville, Texas, Janie's hometown. I'd written to Austin and the headquarters for the Texas Commission on Law Enforcement Standards Education for the chance to challenge the state test. I received the certificate, along with a care package from my longtime friend and fellow Hoosier, the sheriff of Willacy County, Larry Spence.

Larry and I had met back in the middle '70s when he'd come to work for the Willacy County Sheriff's Department as one of their deputies. It resulted in a friendship that has lasted these past forty-three years. Larry hails from Clinton, Indiana. In addition to both of us being Hoosiers, we had both marriage young ladies of Mexican heritage from Raymondville. Larry continues working for the county as it longest-serving sheriff. He is also the chaplain for the Texas Sheriff's Association and a part-time pastor at local protestant services for some of the surrounding churches in the area.

After leaving Chanute in March of 1993, on terminal leave, I spent the next several weeks studying and preparing to take the state test in hopes of being reinstated as a Texas police officer. I was also spending time in San Antonio looking for work. I'd applied for a position with the Bexar County Sheriff's Department. After passing the written test, physical exam, and physical challenges (run, push-ups, etc.) I was told because my eyesight was not 20/80 uncorrected, I was not qualified. I wrote to the newly elected sheriff to complain.

I told Sheriff Lopez I was a newly retired US Air Force Security police officer with bachelor's and master's degrees who was willing to start in the jail at the bottom and work my way up the ladder. I explained that their vision criterion was stricter than the FBI's. A couple of weeks later, I got a call from a female lieutenant in their training division who told me if I could get a doctor to certify at least one eye, they'd hire me. I laughed and told the lieutenant I would not try and get someone to lie in order to satisfy their unduly and asinine vision criterion. If they didn't want to hire me as I was, that was their loss.

My efforts at finding a job in San Antonio were a bust, so I ended up becoming part of the Willacy County Sheriff's Department Reserve Deputy program after passing the state test at the Alamo Police Academy in San Antonio in April of 1993. My retirement from the Air Force became official on June 1, 1993. In hindsight, I realize God's plans for me weren't in San Antonio. No matter what, I was destined to become part of the Valley community again.

Getting back into civilian law enforcement took some adjusting. The culture and lifestyle in South Texas are different than many other places. One of my friends asked me several months after my retirement what living in the Valley was like. I told him it was like living in a third world country that flies the stars and stripes. I know he could not appreciate that comment because he'd never visited let alone spent any time down here in the Rio Grande Valley. The attitude and way of seeing things in South Texas, especially counties like Willacy and Starr, are behind the rest of the country. While many of the community leaders thought they were in the know, they hadn't been any place else to know any better. Willacy County leadership is a great example of people who seem to be stuck in a time warp. It's one of the reasons the county is one of the poorest in Texas. With the current mind-set and leadership that exists in that county, they have little hope for growth and modernization in the future.

Part of the adjustment was the realization that my fellow South Texas cops were totally clueless about the threat posed by terrorists. They didn't have a clear understanding regarding the ever-present illegal crossing of the border by Hispanics from a variety of countries from Mexico to Honduras, El Salvador, Nicaragua, and Costa Rica in Central America to any number of countries in South America, that Middle Eastern terrorist were also embedded among them. It seems the fact that Middle Easterners look more like Latinos than Canadians is missed by the vast majority of Americans. And not just those on our Southern Border.

This is even more apparent today as I listen to the way the media reports what's going on down here on the South Texas-Mexican border, or doesn't report at all. Add to that the completely ignorant knowledge and view of leftist politicians. The left and their buddies in Congress know there's a problem but don't want to admit it because it would bolster President Trump's assertion and the constant declaration that there's a national emergency along our Southern Border.

This includes congressmen Vela, Gonzalez, and Cuellar who have lived a few short miles from the border most of their lives. Collectively, they represent at least three counties that share their borders with Mexico. They choose to follow their party's talking points instead of admitting the truth and working in a bipartisan manner to fix the problems of both immigration and the border wall. Only those of us who live here and have to deal with the problems of illegal aliens on a daily basis understand the true nature of what is taking place.

In January of 1994, I left the Willacy County Sheriff's Department, where I'd worked as a deputy and chief jail administrator for some six months, to assume a new position as the assistant chief of police at UT Pan American. I'd been hired by their chief, Howard Miller, who was from Houston. He had little real experience other than being a security officer at Baylor, even though he claimed to have worked undercover in Harris County as well. After watching and working with him, I have my doubts about voracity of that claim.

While he had a bachelor's degree, he had no administrative experience running a police department and managing people. He was more interested in dressing to the nines as if he'd had stepped off the pages of *GQ* magazine. He never failed to demonstrate his arrogance and dislike for being in the Valley let alone his seeing himself as superior than the rest of us. When he carried a gun, it was always in his briefcase. He never wore it on his person.

His inexperience was immediately apparent by his choice of police cars. He purchased used Department of Public Safety (DPS) vehicles and then complained about the recurring maintenance costs. I told him that's why the DPS auctions off those cars after their troopers run them into the ground. I convinced him we needed to develop a five-year plan whereby we'd purchase a couple of new vehicles each year. These cars would be under warranty. After a few years, we wouldn't have vehicles that were out of warranty, thus eliminating the lion's share of the maintenance costs.

Another area he'd not done well in was communications he'd chosen for the department. The radio would have been great for a taxi company, but not for a police department. UT Pan American had parking enforcement officers, security officers, and police officers. The parking enforcement guys would walk the parking lots writing tickets on violators. They were constantly on the radio, checking on how many previous tickets a particular car might have. If a car had several tickets, they would contact the security guys to bring them tire boots (locks that keep the driver from moving the care).

I explained to the chief this was not a good system. The parking and security officers were constantly tying up the radios, making it very difficult for the commissioned officers to gain access when on calls for service or traffic stops. We needed a system where the parking enforcement and security officer had one channel for their use while the commissioned officer had another for theirs.

Because of the chief's lack of experience as a real police officer, he failed to understand the serious nature of the police officer not being able to get help if it became necessary. He blew me off and said the system would be fine. A few months later, the motor on the library elevator began smoking. Pandemonium and chaos rained down on the campus. The chief couldn't get a clear channel to issue instructions because the parking and security folks had it tied up. I gave him that "I told you so" look. He clearly didn't appreciate it.

During the time frame I was at the campus in my police position, the university was still doing arena registration. This resulted in several hundred thousands of dollars needing to be deposited after hours in the local bank. I established a procedure for an officer to drive the route looking for any suspicious people or vehicles. When that person was satisfied, the unit carrying the money in the trunk would drive to the bank escorted by another marked patrol car. Since the university is less than fifteen miles from the border, prudence dictated caution in money that large sum of money.

The chief didn't see it that way. He said I was overreacting. He didn't feel such precautions were needed. From my perspective, it was another example of his lack of experience in the real world of policing. Thankfully, during my tenure, we did not experience any problems along those lines.

The chief also ignored me when I pointed out his sergeant (of the same last name) was having an affair with one of his subordinates. This was common knowledge among the rest of the officers and security personnel. This same female was later promoted to corporal and placed in charge of the campus Criminal Investigations Division, all the while continuing her illicit affair with a married man. The chief remained clueless.

Over a year later, when I discovered she had been slacking off in her job (I found arrest folders on her desk that had never been turned over the district attorney's office), I began putting pressure on her to do her job. This resulted in her filing sexual harassment charge against me, with the support of her lover. The chief used this to pressure me into resigning.

This was one of those situations where I went through a good deal of depression. I was hurt by the lies and false accusations of these people. This is where the poem about the footprints in the sand was right on point. My ability and faith in knowing God was there for me, coupled with the strong and loving support of my wife and family, made all the difference in me slowing bouncing back.

Situations like this help a person to understand the emotional turmoil that takes place when they are falsely accused and lied about. For politicians and others whose situations are played out in the media, it is many times more difficult. I can't imagine having to deal with media types camping out in front of my house and pestering my neighbors and loved ones. They are so consumed with getting the story they conduct themselves with no respect, empathy, or understanding with regard to what the person and their family is going through. They are like a swarm of piranhas attacking a side of beef.

I found out later the sergeant had divorced his wife and married the corporal. Either the chief was too stupid to realize what was going on, or he was a part of it. What was also clear by the corporal's actions, both when she worked at the Hidalgo County Sheriff's Department and for the UT Pan American police, was her deceptiveness in dealing with people and the truth. She had no problem lying or establishing false accusations if it got her out of trouble or something she wanted. When she worked at the sheriff's department, she was having an affair with the sheriff's brother, another married man. She got pregnant from that relationship, only to turn around and accuse him of sexual harassment.

Politics around the campus was ever present. Whether it was the chief's boss (an arrogant guy named Langebeer who had once introduced Miller, who is very black in color, to smile so everyone could see him) or some high-and-mighty professor, my officers and I always had to walk on eggshells. It was frustrating having to deal with men and women who had earned a PhD and thought they were the most intelligent people in the world. The vast majority of them had never been anywhere other than some academic campus. They had no real-world experiences or knowledge yet allowed their arrogance and narcissism to look down on the rest of us. After all that education, you would have thought someone would have taught them in order to earn respect, you have to give it. In fairness, I do know quite a few PhDs who are truly genuine and down-to-earth people.

After two and a half years of dealing working in this atmosphere and telling the chief I would not falsify records for him because he didn't want to undergo training in a particular area like weapons qualification, coupled with the false accusations of sexual harassment, I called it quits. I didn't need people so lacking in integrity and honor impugning mine any further.

Experimenting with Other Careers

The political hassles and small-minded potentates I'd begun coming across since retiring, both in Willacy County and the university, left me with a bitter taste in my mouth. Sheriff Spence put me back on as a reserve deputy. This helped me keep my police license alive. I started looking around for something different to do. This led me to sell cars for a couple of months.

I was hired by the Bert Ogden car dealership on Jackson and Hackberry Streets to sell Nissans and Oldsmobiles. They also sold BMWs there, but I wasn't seasoned (their words) enough to sell them according to their leadership. I did that for two months and left to sell new homes for Kimball Hill.

Selling new cars involved long boring hours waiting for people to walk into the showroom. Initially, there were hours of studying and learning about the cars we sold. You worked sixty to eighty hours a week and didn't get paid much when you sold a car. What you did get paid was minimum wage. The markup and money was in selling used vehicles. Only the sales folks who'd been around a while got to sell those.

While I learned a lot about the car business and became knowledgeable about what I was selling, I also learned you lived from one sale to the next. As a person who had gone through much in life with either an hourly wage or a salary, wondering if you would make enough sales to pay the bills each week was not my idea of fun. It brought about a level of stress I'd never known because I always knew what I was being paid each pay period.

I sold homes for Kimball Hill for a year. Here again you were sitting around, waiting for people to visit the show home, just like in the dealership. You had to find out how serious they were about buying a new home. More importantly, you had to determine if they could afford one. While I enjoyed working with customers in designing and choosing a particular floor plan, I was still not finding myself doing what really satisfied me.

While selling homes, I began taking classes from South Texas Community College (later to become South Texas College). I took biology, anatomy, and physiology, along with EMT basic and intermediate courses. Over the period of the fall of 1996 and spring of 1997 semesters, I took twenty-nine hours and was on the dean's list with a straight 4.0 grade point average both semesters. Boy would my mom have been surprised. Who knew? I guess as I matured and learned more about myself and life, I also developed a greater appreciation for education and knowledge.

After leaving Kimball Hill, I tried working for a company that sold whole house water treatment systems. Toward the end, I had invested in the company and became its owner. After a few short months, I was forced to shut it down because of my rising debt.

The markup of the product was good. The people we did in home demos for by and large couldn't afford the system. I was surprised by the number of people who wanted to finance the systems, only to find out their finances and credit score was in the toilet. The picture of people in South Texas and their lack of concern over their own financial instabilities were sad. I attribute much of this to ignorance and poor upbringing by their parents.

After closing the business, I went for a few weeks trying to find a job. All too often, I heard the same comment: "You're overqualified." I ended up qualifying for government assistance to attend truck driver's school since I hadn't earned a paycheck in several months.

I drove to San Antonio to attend the school for three weeks. I still had feelers out for work in the valley. By the end of the third week, I'd been advised by a fellow retired Air Force major named Mario Reyna (now the dean of Business, Public Safety, and Technology at South Texas College) that there was a Department of Labor grant position as director opening up.

I applied and was hired just after passing my commercial driver's test in San Antonio and receiving a job offer from the trucking company USA out of Arkansas. I sure would have been one well-educated trucker. I was asked by a friend why I'd agreed to drive semi-tractor trailers across the country. I told him it was honest work that paid well, and it beat flipping burgers.

After undergoing the in-processing paperwork and being assigned my work location, I was briefed about what the job would entail. My title was director of the O'Net grant. The focus of the grant was to create a curriculum that would provide training to unemployed individuals in one of the various factories located south of McAllen, Texas, just north of Hidalgo and its port of entry into and out of Mexico. The grant was to be for one year; however, we were able to secure an extension for a second.

The process started with me attending a course entitled DACUM, an acronym for Develop a Curriculum. Once I had completed the course, we set out to find a company who would hire those people we trained. We found a company that produced plastic parts via the plastic mold injection process. Next, we acquired the service of people considered to be subject matter experts (SMEs) in this field. Through a week of questions and answers, we put together a basic curriculum, along with the minimum criteria potential students would have to meet. This included minimum English (speaking and reading comprehension) and math skills. Then we set out to advertise and begin the selection process.

I was saddened by the poor quality of candidates we received. For every ten people we interviewed, we'd find one that met these minimum standards. As time went along, I found this was the norm in the Rio Grande Valley. There were a lot of illegal aliens, along with others of Mexican heritage, who were poorly educated, if at all. Once the requisite number of people were selected, we conducted the first class. Overall, we trained approximately thirty-two men and women.

Prior to these people being accepted, they were taken for an interview with the company. The company had agreed to hire our candidates once they successfully completed the training. These people were also given a complete tour of the factory and shown every aspect of what the job involved. Nothing was left to chance before the deal was made. We also helped them with transportation and childcare as the need dictated.

After three classes of students had been trained and were on the job, we went back a few months later to follow up. What we found was disappointing, to say the least. Two had returned to work with former employers. One had gotten a better job with another company. A few were still working for the original company. But the majority, more than twenty-five, had just stopped showing up.

We began making contact with these people and asking them why they were no longer working at the company. Many said they didn't like the work. Still, others complained about too much time on their feet. What we discovered was interesting as well as telling. Those still working had worked with other companies in the Valley like Hager or Levi Strauss. When the companies closed, they were laid off. These people were anxious to find a job and eagerly jumped at the opportunity to train for a new one.

The ones who had just stopped showing up had never held a job before. They came from families that had been on welfare for two or more generations. They didn't know how to work. Worse, they liked taking money from the government. While welfare wasn't a lot of money, it was still free and had no job requirements. These welfare recipients were the product of Johnson's Great Society Bill in 1964. The then-president's idea of how to eradicate poverty. What a joke.

The lesson was clear. There are those who willingly do not want to work. They wish only to take handouts from the government, our tax dollars, and live with no responsibilities. This is supported by Democrats who see these people as pawns who will keep them in office because they want to continue getting the free handouts. There should be work requirements, drug testing, and monitoring before these people should be allowed to collect any welfare money or assistance. These people should also receive some type of training or education and then be required to go to work. Sadly, our politicians don't seem to care. Even in the Bible, God tells us, "If a man will not work, neither shall he eat" (2 Thessalonians 3:10).

During the two years I functioned as the director of the grant, I became involved with the political science department. Its chair at the time was Paul Hernandez, chaired both the government and criminal justice (CJ) departments. I'd paid him a visit as I was interested in being one of his adjuncts for his CJ program. Paul advised me he had plenty of folks to teach part-time in that area but was hurting for adjuncts to teach government. He asked me about my master's degree. I told him it was in international relations. He asked me to bring in my college transcript so we could look it over. Once I did, we found I had over twenty hours that qualified as political science. Shortly after that, I began teaching three classes a semester and during summer sessions.

Remember, up to this point, my only involvement with politics was the frustration of Clinton becoming president because of the way he described his feeling about the military. As I began teaching high school seniors, who were receiving both high school and college credit for my class, I began to develop a clearer understanding of our government and how this country came to be. I also started to familiarize myself with the people who were running our country. The more I learned, the less I liked what I was seeing.

After completing the two year grant I was once again retired. I was made aware of a teaching position that was opening up at Texas State Technical College later the Spring of 2001. I applied for the job and was hired. My primary duties were to teach American and Texas Government classes to high school seniors via their "Distance Learning Program." This entailed me sitting in a studio and teaching classes to students in three of four different high schools located in Harlingen, where I lived, as well as in three other cities. I started in this position in the Fall of 2001 and remained there until retiring in May of 2013. I taught three distance learning classes during the week as well as a class on Tuesday and Thursday afternoons, and Saturday mornings.

When I first started teaching in the Fall of 2001 Janie and I were living in McAllen, Texas. I drove daily the forty or so miles back and forth six days a week. I took advantage of the time to listen to "Books on Tape." This allowed me to basically review a number of books on political subjects, thus enhancing my knowledge and understanding of the issues and problems America was experiencing, and the politicians who were on opposite sides of the problems from each other.

The college wanted me to teach in the summer, but I chose not to. During several of the summers I drove up to my old alma mater, Culver Military Academy to work at their annual summer camps. The camps were six weeks long and consisted of an upper and lower camp. The lower camp was for children from nine to thirteen years of age. The upper camp was for older kids from thirteen to seventeen years of age.

Staff reported to the academy at least a week in advance for training and to prepare their respective areas for the arrival of the campers. Two summers I was the senior counselor for Naval Company Two. One summer I inaugurated a new self-defense program. And three summers I was the director of their rifle range and marksmanship program.

The summer I was able to work at Culver provided some of my best memories, especially being the senior counselor to seventy-two boys from thirteen to seventeen years of age. I had a small apartment in the barracks with the campers. I lived and worked with them twenty-four hours a day, seven days a week for the duration of the camp. Like the director told us upon being hired to that position, "this will be the toughest job you'll ever love."

During these years, 1994 to 2017, I continued teaching karate at different locations, representing the AKS, writing articles on the martial arts for the AKS newsletter and various publication, as well as traveling to Germany on two different occasions (June of 2011 and September of 2014) to conduct seminars and serve as the president of the testing board. Having had to retire due to health was a bitter pill. The friendships and memories I have are forever with me.

My Political Education

To this point, you have hopefully developed some idea about the kind of person I am and how God's hand has continuously been a part of my life, shaping both my personal and political views. I don't consider myself anyone great or extraordinary. Merely a man who has traveled the path God has shown him as best I could. I've made my share of mistakes as all of us have and do. Like any sinner, we realize this is who we are. We also realize the great love and blessings that God has shown us by sending His Son to suffer and die on the cross so that we might have everlasting life. The key is in what we learned from mistakes and how you proceed forward. I know other Christians fully understand what I'm talking about.

Watching the transformation of the Democratic Party go from a national one to a socialist one over the past several decades has been truly interesting, while at the same time sad. The Democratic Party is no longer the party of Roosevelt, Truman, Kennedy, and other Christian politicians who proudly declared themselves Democrats. In those days, Democrats and Republicans argued over domestic issues but stood shoulder to shoulder at the edge of the shore when it came to the defense and protection of our country.

Today's Democratic Party has become one full of radical leftists and hard-core socialists. Some, like John Brennan, even voted for Communists. What's truly sad about this is the fact that Brennan was the director of the CIA and national defense advisor to Obama. Obviously, because of Obama's far-left leanings, he wasn't concerned with placing a Communist sympathizer in such sensitive positions. We must never lose sight of the fact that these people care not one whiff for your opinion or that of anyone else's if it doesn't fit their narrative and agenda. Their desire is to create a big government by which they can control us all.

The late Senator Zell Miller from Georgia even wrote a book about it entitled *National Party No More*. As a lifelong card-carrying Democrat, Miller saw that partisanship had overcome patriotism in his party. This caused him a great deal of frustration. This, coupled with a deep and burning loathing on the part of many in the Democratic Party, and to some extent among some deep state Republicans for the current president Donald Trump, has given us a nonfunctional government. In a way, that might be a good thing.

So deep is the hatred on the part of Speaker Pelosi (and the vast majority of those on the left) that she would not negotiate with the president on a wall or barrier to protect our country from the illegal aliens pouring over it. Even though previous Presidents Bush, Clinton, and Obama had pushed for the wall, she preferred to do everything in her power to keep Trump from doing what was needed to protect our country. There was no way she would relent and give Trump the money for that project.

The irony of all this is that over the past year or so, the amount of money that has and is being spent to house, transport, and care for these illegal aliens could have more than paid for the wall.

Pelosi and her ilk only care about obstructing Trump's presidency and getting him removed from office by any means. That's why you hear idiots like Maxine Waters, Jerry Nadler, Adam Schiff, and the rest of these people constantly braying about impeachment. Pelosi's hatred and vindictiveness have blinded her to the people's business and the safety and security of our nation. They have also disrespected the election results. The people voted, and Trump won. That's not good enough for the poor losers in the Democratic Party or their left-wing supporters. The will of the people be damned.

This is clearly evident in the nearly two years (675 days) Mueller spent investigating absolutely nothing. We're now finding out he knew there was no collusion a few months after being appointed as the special counsel. More than thirty-eight million dollars has been spent. Nineteen anti-Trump lawyers were employed. More than five hundred search warrants issued. And a host of FBI agents were used—all for nothing.

This picture was taken in Mulehausen Germany in September of 2014. Pictured from left to right are Jude Gore from West Virginia, AKS 7th Dan, me, Werner Sigmund, Heinrich Reimer AKS 8th Dan, Franke Sigmund AKS 6th Dan (just promoted), Katrina Franke's wife, and Andreas Modl AKS 7th Dan. Andreas is the sole individual responsible for establishing the AKS as an officially recognized martial arts style in the German Karate Union

The now-released Mueller report clearly states there was no collusion. And yet the Democrats still refuse to admit there was no collusion or obstruction. Even the *New York Times* has finally admitted the Steele Dossier was a fake. This was the document paid and supported by the Clintons and Democratic Party. This same document was used to falsely acquire FISA warrants (special secret warrants signed by federal judges to spy on Americans). Now we also find out Mueller knew this all along. How truly culpable are the Democrats in this whole sorted affair?

What this has clearly been was an all-out full-court effort on the part of the Clintons, the Obama administration, and Democrats in general to overturn a duly elected president. In a word, this was a political coup d'état. A political hit job by a group of people who were not happy with the election results because they lost. The more that evidence about things like "spying" comes out, the clearer the picture of these liberals' involvement becomes.

For all the accolades and praise that has been heaped on Mueller, the truth is simple. It's based off the facts and his conduct over this whole affair. He is a partisan hack who has made a mockery out of our government, the justice system, and the political process this country has followed for more than two hundred years to elect our presidents. Mueller is a pawn of the left and has been doing their bidding since assuming the special counsel position. From my standpoint, he does not deserve praise; he deserves our disdain. He has been a willing co-conspirator with key people in the justice department, the FBI, the DNC, and the Clintons who financed the whole thing. It is my sincere hope those who are guilty will be judged and go to prison. Nothing short of this will be acceptable.

Defining the True Nature of Leftists, Democrats and Politicians

For everyone's general edification, and due to the fact too many high school (and in some cases college) graduates have such a poor vocabulary, I want to describe some words that are germane to the current efforts and mind-sets of those on the left and in the Democratic Party, and to some extent in the Republican party as well (the never Trumpers). Think about the meanings/definitions of these words and see how closely they apply today to the majority on the left and especially the Democratic Party.

The first is *fascism*. This is a form of radical authoritarian ultra-nationalism, characterized by dictatorial power, *forcible suppression of opposition* (like what is going on our college and university campuses), and strong regimentation of society and of the economy, which came into prominence in early twentieth century.

Second, we have *oligarchy*. This is a form of power structure in which power rests with a small number of people. These people may be distinguished by nobility, wealth, family ties, education or corporate, religious, political, or military control.

Lastly is an *aristocracy*. This is a form of government that places strength in the hands of a small, *privileged ruling class* (much like we see being attempted by the left in their desire to create a strong central government from which all aspects of the means of production and our lives are controlled). This word comes from the Greek *aristokratia*, meaning "rule of the best-born." This was also one of the main goals of Margret Sanger and her application of eugenics.

I provide these three definitions because there are currently in Congress and among their hard-core followers on the left, those who fit parts of each of these definitions. They are arrogant beyond description and willing to break any law if it furthers their agenda (e.g., the Clintons). No longer is the rule of law with these people important. No longer does due process count. No longer do First Amendment rights or freedom of speech matter. They define what's right at the time and with the situation at hand. It's all about what they say it is in order to get their way. Their moto should be, "Do as I say, not as I do."

Some other words that should be understood when observing politicians (and many in Hollywood) and their ilk are the following:

Arrogance, the quality of being arrogant. "The arrogance of this man is astounding."
Synonyms: *haughtiness, conceit, hubris, self-importance, egotism, sense of superiority*
Noun—excessive interest in or admiration of oneself and one's physical appearance.
Synonyms: *vanity, self-love, self-admiration, self-adulation, self-absorption, self-obsession, conceit, self-conceit, self-centeredness, self-regard, egotism, egoism, egocentricity, egomania*

Psychology of Arrogance

Selfishness, involving a sense of entitlement, a lack of empathy, and a need for admiration as characterizing a personality type. This also describes many of today's millennials. These young people believe the government owes them a free education, free health care, housing, and a job. They lack any true understanding of reality. This is part and parcel of the socialist movement so many of them escribe too.

Psychoanalysis of Arrogance

Self-centeredness arising from failure to distinguish the self from external objects, either in very young babies or as a feature of mental disorder.

> Noun: *Narcissist*—a person who has an excessive interest in or admiration of themselves.

> "Narcissists think the world revolves around them."

> Definition: The hallmarks of narcissistic personality disorder (NPD) are grandiosity, a lack of empathy for other people, and a need for admiration. People with this condition are frequently described as arrogant, self-centered, manipu-

lative, and demanding (someone running for president?).

The National Institute of Mental Health (NIMH) defines someone who is "psychotic" as out of touch with reality, likely experiencing false beliefs, known as delusions, or false sights or sounds, known as hallucinations. (Democrats always claiming they're doing what Americans want. What percentage? Without a doubt only about 25 percent.)

Other words you should be aware of are *envy* and *covet*. I mentioned the "politics of envy" earlier. You must know the term *envy* plays a key role in the true nature of what makes liberals tick, as does their desire to have what others have without working to earn it. *Envy* is described by *Wikipedia* as (from Latin *invidia*) an emotion that "occurs when a person lacks another's superior quality, achievement, or possession and either desire it or wishes that the other lacked it." (wow. For me, that hits the nail on the head when talking about the current crop of millennial liberals.)

The other word I gave you was to *covet*. Definition of *coveting* (transitive verb):

> 1: To wish for or earnestly covet an award; 2: to desire (what belongs to another) inordinately or culpably (this means with criminal intent to take it). The king's brother coveted the throne.
> Intransitive verb: to feel an inordinate desire for what belongs to another.

The last word you should be familiar with is *demagogue*. Here's the definition of the word and some examples of how it's used. Politicians are notorious for getting on their soapboxes in front of cameras or while standing in the well of either chamber of the House or Senate so they can pontificate and act like the issue is something they really care about.

dem·a·gogue: /ˈdeməˌgäg/ *noun*

A political leader who seeks support by appealing to the desires and prejudices of ordinary people rather than by using rational argument. "A gifted demagogue with particular skill in manipulating the press."

synonyms: rabble-rouser, political agitator, agitator, soapbox orator, firebrand

Verb, US, Rhetorically exploit (an issue) for political purposes in a way calculated to appeal to the desires and prejudices of ordinary people. "He seems more interested in demagoguing the issue in media interviews than in dialogue."

When you look at how politicians (and many of their supporters) conduct themselves, coupled with how they treat people (especially their congressional staffs when the TV cameras are not rolling), these definitions become clear. Are these really the people we want representing us as citizens, or even better, representing our country to the rest of the world?

As a Christian, the attitudes and very conduct of these people violate a variety of the teaching taught in the bible as well as the Ten Commandments our Lord handed down to Moses. I truly feel since the elimination of prayer in our schools along with the reading of the Bible, and even the mere presence of the Ten Commandments hanging on the wall, in the 1962–63 time frame was the beginning of our country's downhill slide into its current state of sinfulness and utter lack of respectable moral conduct.

Liberal vs. Conservative

During the years I taught American and Texas government, I had students ask me what the difference was between Democrats and Republicans (liberals vs. conservatives). I was always happy when a young male or female student ask that question for two reasons. First, it demonstrated to me they really didn't understand the terms and their corresponding concepts/ideologies. Secondly, they were willing to risk embarrassing themselves (some felt it was a stupid question) because they wanted to understand these terms as they applied to our political system and way of thinking. I would thank them for being brave and inquisitive enough to want to know. I further explained to them there is no such thing as a stupid question. If you don't know something, not asking questions that will result in you understanding is stupid.

I explained that conservatives are people who believe in the greatness of this country and the founding documents (Declaration of Independence, Constitution, and Bill of Rights) that helped shape it. That means ensuring we elect politicians and appoint judges who are originalists (keeping our founding documents as they are without revision or deletion). Conservatives do not believe in big government, excessive taxation, or free handouts to those who could and should be working to support themselves and their families as contributing members of our society. They also don't believe in regulations that stifle progress. Conservatives do believe in a strong military that will protect us.

They believe our government should be fiscally responsible and live within a set budget. Conservatives believe our capitalistic system is the engine that fuels our progress. They also believe people should be left alone and allowed to succeed on their own in life. Clearly, those who have good work habits and ethics, coupled with a strong drive and motivation, are successful. Above all, conservatives believe in the rule of law. These are found in the founding documents I've previously mentioned, as well as the penal codes and other statutes that form the heart and soul of our legal system.

Liberals, on the other hand, want to control our lives through an intrusive big government that establishes laws for the purpose of controlling how we live and what we are and are not allowed to do. These laws (rules) are ones leftists view as necessary to keep people from doing things those on the left disagree with. This includes things as simple as certain foods and quantities of drink containers. Even whether you should be allowed to use straws with your drinks.

In order to support the government and all the (allegedly) free programs they want to establish, liberals have to impose heavy taxation. They see the money (our tax dollars) paid to the government as theirs, to do with as they see fit. They don't support a strong military and try to control all aspects of our society through repressive and harsh regulations. Their supporters like to protest and get in people's faces. They use the vilest of language and do not respect anyone but themselves. They border on anarchy in some cases.

Liberals believe in equality across the board. They feel when someone has too much money of other possessions, they need to be taxed heavier in order to give that person's money (wealth) to those who've done nothing to earn it. All one need do is look at the "New Green Deal" Alexandria Ocascio-Cortez and her far-left socialists are pushing to understand what I've just said. They don't care if the person earned what they have through their own sweat and toil. They want to take it away so they can "redistribute" it to those who have less.

Liberals and the Democratic Party are people who are jealous of people who are successful and happy. Remember those terms *envy* and *covet*? They're always preaching tax the rich when they themselves are multimillionaires (that's why the Senate is called the millionaires' club). They stand on their soapboxes, spewing their rhetoric of class envy because it appeals to young people who have yet to earn their way in life, let alone being able to understand its realities. It also appeals to adults who will never be a success because they lack the drive and motivation it takes to succeed. Here again, the idea of getting something for nothing is very appealing. While this latter group may lack what it takes to be better off, they are still envious of those who have what they'd like to have. Such is the nature of socialism. To pit the haves against the have-nots. The rich against the poor. Class envy. It is the mechanism democrats have used for the past fifty plus years to divide us as a people.

I used this story a colleague shared with me one time in an effort to get my students to understand the difference between the social-ist ideologies and those of conservatives. It involves a father whose daughter was a junior in college and had very liberal views. She was always talking about people had too much of one thing or another and should be required to share with others. Since his daughter was a straight A student, he asked her how her friend Jessica was doing in school. The daughter explained how she is always studying and working hard to pass tests and write research papers while Jessica missed classes all the time, partied a lot, and is one of the more pop-ular girls on campus. The daughter told her dad she had to work hard in order to maintain her 4.0 grade average. Jessica, on the other hand, was barely maintaining a 2.0 average.

The father suggested to his daughter, since she felt so strongly about equality and sharing with those who had less or weren't doing as well, she should go down to the dean's offices and have them take a point off her grade average in order to give it to Jessica. That way, they'd both have the same 3.0 grade average, and everything would be fair and equal. The daughter flew out of her chair, yelling about how hard she has had to work to maintain her grade average. She said it wouldn't be fair because she worked so hard for her grades while Jessica partied all the time. It wouldn't be fair for her to give up a grade point to Jessica so they could be equal. Jessica hasn't done what it takes to deserve a higher grade average. Her dad smiled and responded, "Welcome to the Conservative movement."

This little story highlights the key differences between social-ists/liberals and conservatives. Most people work very hard for what they earn in life. No one has the right to tell them they have to give up a certain portion of that to others who haven't worked as hard or made the same sacrifices. It's for this reason those of us who have struggled our entire lives to earn a living for our families and prepare to enjoy a comfortable retirement resent the government taking our tax dollars in order to give the money to those who've chosen not to work. These are people who have no honor or self-respect. To give money to those who are not willing to earn it the honest way through an honest day's labor is wrong.

Most liberal politicians are well off financially and don't need the handouts. They use this ploy of taking from the rich to give to the poor because it gets votes from the people who enjoy collecting welfare and not having to work for what they get. Democrats will do and say virtually anything to stay in power so they can control how the rest of us live.

The Failure of Modern-Day Education

The other day, I was visiting with my fourteen-year-old grandson. I asked him if he had ever heard about the Berlin Wall. He told me the only wall his teachers talked about was the one Trump wanted to build. This comment clearly highlights the major problem we have in our country. Teachers no longer teach about the founders, our revolution against England, our Declaration of Independence, and how our Constitution and Bill of Rights came to be.

Today's teachers have been indoctrinated during their college and university studies by liberal socialist professors. In some cases, their professor believes more in communism than the capitalism that made this country the powerhouse it is in the world. Teachers now inject their personal political beliefs in their classes. Their students know little to nothing about politics and are completely trusting (gullible) of their teachers because they don't know any better. These teachers are no longer teaching. They have become propagandists.

When this country is eventually destroyed from within by liberalism and socialism, those who have been teachers pushing this ideologies will be as guilty of ruining this great nation as the ones who eventually bring it down. There is no escaping this reality.

Now, in all fairness, there are still some great teachers and educational institutions like Hillsdale College and Liberty University. They both make an honest effort at teaching our country's history without distortion or revision. There are also other schools and institutions that are faith based that also do a good job at teaching the truth about our country and its founding.

As a lifelong teacher (martial arts, American and Texas government, and criminal justice), one of the key things I learned early on is the importance of mentoring and challenging student to apply critical thinking. People who teach are given a big responsibility. They have taken on this responsibility in order educate people. Not fill them full of the teacher's own biases.

It was important for me to teach my students about our Declaration of Independence, the Constitution, and our Bill of Rights. I felt it was important for them to understand why this nation was started and how it has evolved, both the good and the bad. When students finished the end of the semester, they took away with them a much better appreciation of what the pioneers and founders of this country endured in order to eventually succeed. I didn't talk about how bad they were because many of them were slave owners or the injustices that were perpetrated upon the American Indians. Judging people who lived over a hundred and fifty to two hundred plus years ago by today's standards is the height of arrogance on one side and pure ignorance on the other.

For me, it was God placing me in a position where I could both mentor and minister. I can't begin to tell you how many young people came to me with problems. I felt blessed that God had steered them to me. Over the years, since retiring from the classroom, I've had people approach me who were once students of mine. They thanked me for helping them develop a better understanding of our government and how it's supposed to work. They've thanked me for being objective and open-minded in order for the class to be able to engage in truly open and honest dialogues regarding a number of subjects.

I've had the same experience from the karate classes I taught. One student in particular had studied with me in Edinburg for four years while he attended high school. He was ready to test for his first degree black belt. After he graduated, he went to work for the local grocery store in town—HEB. After high school, he married his high school sweetheart, Bea.

David approached me one day and told me he's been selected to join the US Border Patrol. He was nervous about the prospect and asked me what I thought. I told him it was a great opportunity. If he walked through that door, the sky was the limit. He joined and some twenty-eight years later became the chief of the United States Border Patrol. David Aguilar was a true example of a small-town boy realizing the American dream.

After reconnecting in 2007, I ask David if he would be available to speak with student from my class and anyone else at the college interested in attending. Chief Aguilar was coming to the Valley to perform a change of command ceremony. The ceremony was to be held at the Marine Military Academy that sits adjacent to the campus. The occasion was to install Ron Vitalli as the new chief of the South Texas southern area.

As we planned the visit, I spoke with his aide Tim Sullivan. Tim asked me what it was I wanted the chief to speak about. I told him he could speak about those areas the Border Patrol were engaged in along our border with Mexico, but I was more interested in David speaking to the students, more than 85 percent Mexican American, about being able to fulfill the American dream.

David had grown up alongside many well-known Valley Chicanos who had also become successful in other areas. Because of David's background, he was the perfect person to speak to these young people and challenge them to strive for success in their respective lives. He was a great role model and example.

The day of the visit arrived, and David spoke for nearly an hour. During that time, he expressed to the collective group the positive impact I'd had on him during the years he studied with me. I was humbled beyond words and had to fight back the tears.

It's experiences like this that make teaching so rewarding. Knowing you've truly touched a life in a positive way. For me, this has also meant sharing my faith.

Also part of modern day education can be seen in the attitudes of people who, for lack of a better way to say it, hate the country they were born in. Why do I say that? I say that simply because they no longer look at our history for a better understanding of the struggles early Americans endured. They no longer see how this country started a whole new way of life and government. A government based on the concept of one of the people, for the people and by the people. Ours is not a government run by an aristocracy or a monarchy as was the case for so many centuries.

Now they denigrate and disrespect the founding fathers because they were slave owners. They focus on the treatment of the Indians as settlers moved west ward. In short today's teachers teach their students that the United States is not an honorable country because of all the bad things it's people have done to others over the years. These teachers (secondary, under graduate and graduate) and their students now disrespect the country of their birth as they judge those of past generations by today's standards of ethics and conduct. Of course it's their idea of ethics and conduct with no consideration to the difference in the cultures from one era to the next. For my part I see these people as arrogant because they choose to judge others by their views on life in today's world.

The Early Desires for Freedom from Oppression

(Taken from the *American Freedoms Primer*,
by Adams, pages 5–11)

The desire on man's part for freedom from oppression goes back centuries. The first foundation stone laid was the Magna Carta of 1215. I had the distinct honor of seeing one of the remaining originals in person in the fall of 1985. It was on display in the Cathedral in Salisbury, England.

This was a proclamation by King John granting certain new rights his barons had pressured him into granting. The importance of the Magna Carta was that is announced the rule of law. It also was the beginning of the transformation of England from a monarchy to representative democracy. A key paragraph of that document reads:

> *No free man shall be taken or imprisoned or dispossessed, or outlawed, or banished, or in any way destroyed, nor will we go upon him, nor send upon him, except by the legal judgment of his peers or by the law of the land.*

In other words, the concept of "due process" was established.

Some four hundred years later, the seeds of the Magna Carta bore fruit in the form of 1628 Petition of Right, and later the 1689 Declaration of Rights. The first document was drafted by the English

Parliament and presented to King Charles I in 1628. This Petition of Right declared the rule of law over the wishes of the king, thus rejecting the doctrine known as divine rights of kings. That is the concept that kings were given their right to rule directly from God. Key among the provisions of this petition were that prisoners committed to jail by the king were to be freed on bail until their trial. The quartering of military personnel in private homes was no longer legal. And civilians could not be tried under martial law. This established certain essential freedoms (personal liberties) for the English people.

King Charles was forced to accept the Petition of Right in order to maintain the support and cooperation of the parliament, without whom he would have difficulty raising funds. Sadly, as history tells us, Charles had no intention of living by the petition. This resulted in the English Civil War of 1642. King Charles lost the war, was convicted of treason, and beheaded.

In 1689, under the new King and Queen William and Mary, Parliament drafted the English Bill of Rights. This document, later established in statutory form, reaffirmed the principles set forth by the Petition of Right. Here again, the declaration set forth protections for the people. They were given religious freedom to be able to dissent (disagree). Judges were made independent. Time limits were set on Parliament (something we need on our congress—term limits). The press was provided protection and freedom to operate openly. It also provides the law that established a representative system of government. The Magna Carta, the Petition of Right, and the Declaration of Rights were the key cornerstones that established the rule of law and English liberties.

Several English writers wrote about the freedoms and liberties set forth by those key documents. Key among them were Algernon Sydney, Edmund Burke, and John Locke. Locke's second treatise, Of Civil Government, provided concepts on social contract theory that was discussed and debated throughout the American Revolution.

Mr. Locke believed that by nature, people had certain rights and duties. Among them were life, liberty, and the right of property ownership. He also put forth the concept that those who ruled did so with the consent of the governed. The people entered into a contract with the government. If the government failed to live up to the contract, the people could dissolve it (the government) and create a new one. In other words, the people were superior to the government. No doubt today's big government liberal Democrats don't like this. What liberals fail to understand, that is clearly stated by Locke, is that governments derive their power and authority from the governed. In other words, from the consent of the people.

When one analyzes our Declaration of Independence, we see the first part is the colonies' justification to the rest of the world for their decision to separate from England and create their own country. The middle part of the document lays out some eighteen grievances held by the colonies toward the crown. The third and last part was the clear and unmistakable wording declaring the creation of the United States and its separation from England that followed Locke's philosophy. In the eyes of the colonies, Britain had not lived up to its end of the contract. Therefore the colonies declared themselves free and independent.

Once this was accomplished, the newly minted United States went full bore into prosecuting the war against England. They also established the Articles of Confederation. Because the former colonies resented the control placed upon them by the crown, they didn't want to replace the crown with another form of the central government. Under the articles, each state was free and separate from the other and was more powerful than the central government.

Unfortunately, the articles gave the central government little to no control, thus resulting in each state coining its own money, establishing trade laws, and other barriers against their neighbors. There is much more to the overall problems the newly formed country was experiencing; key among them being unity or agreement among the states.

The central government couldn't even get enough representatives from their member states to meet in order to amend the articles, which required all thirteen states. Just to conduct normal business required a super majority of nine states. This ultimately led to the realization by the founders that a better form of government was needed. They went to work drafting our present Constitution.

Once the new Constitution was written, there were arguments between two opposing groups. These were the federalists and the anti-federalists. The federalists wanted to ratify the new constitution as it was. The anti-federalists wanted civil liberties, protections for the citizens. One might say these two groups were today's big government Democrats the Federalists, and the more conservative Republicans the anti-federalists. If you are truly interested in the content of the debates over this, one has only to read the *Federalist Papers* to gain a greater understanding.

In the end, an agreement was made between the two groups that the first order of business would be to set down the protections the anti-federalists wanted as the first amendments to the new Constitution. These amendments are now known as our Bill of Rights.

Even today, there is not one word to be found in our Constitution or Bill of Rights that guarantees a free education, a guaranteed income, free housing, free medical care, or any of the myriad of other free things current-day liberal socialists like to tell us we're due. Somebody should really get them to stop smoking so much "gangue" weed.

Part of the new mode of governing under the new Constitution was the concept of federalism. Under federalism, power was divided between the national government and the individual states. Under this concept, the national government was to focus only on those issues that affected the country as a whole. Otherwise, it was the purview and responsibility of each state to be responsible for handling their own business. This idea of federalism and state's rights was so important that it was expressed clearly in the Tenth Amendment.

Amendment X: Those powers not delegated to the United States by the Constitution, nor prohibited by it to the States, are reserved to the States respectively, or to the people.

This is also where the founders included the states in the electoral process of the presidency. First, you have the popular vote, which as we saw in both the 2000 and 2016 elections was won by the Democratic candidate. Secondly, you have the Electoral College. The founders created the Electoral College for two reasons. First, it was to give the states a role in the selection of the president. Second, it was to protect us from mob rule taking over and skewing the election. This has resulted in these two elections because of the populations of California and other large metropolitan cities being largely liberal. Because the left lost both of those elections they want to eliminate the Electoral College. It would seem when poor losers can't win by playing by the rules, they decide it's time to change the rules.

In today's governmental environment, Democrats want the national government to oversee virtually all aspects of American life and the running of the country. They don't want to give state governments that much control over how they handle state business. While a communist system would control and own everything, a socialist system seeks to control as much as possible, without taking away people's rights to property ownership or their ability to make money in a free-market capitalistic system, albeit a heavily taxed one. They have to have some means to collect taxes in order to pay for all the free stuff they wish to shower on everyone.

If you've been paying attention to Ocasio-Cortez's Green Program, you know exactly what I'm talking about. There are more than a dozen and a half so-called Democratic candidates for the 2020 presidential race who have also signed on to this huge desire to have the federal government take over our country. Here, again, the difference between tax-and-spend liberals and most conservatives.

Socialists desire to provide free health care and education, as a minimum, to all. But they never truly take into consideration nor can they adequately explain where that money will come from. The left loves to say they want to tax the rich or the top 1 percent. Even if they taxed them at 100 percent, they would be far short of the actual cost of providing all that free stuff. The money has to come from the taxation of everyone, not just the rich.

The late Margret Thatcher (former prime minister of England) once stated, "Socialism is great until you run out of other people's money." Therein lies the rub. The late Winston Churchill said, "Socialism is a philosophy of failure, the creed of ignorance, and the gospel of envy, its inherent virtue is the equal sharing of misery." To pay for the programs socialists want to generously delve out, they have to get it from taxpaying citizens, companies and corporations, import/export fees, and tariffs, to name but a few of the types of taxes they will levy on us. The government, on its own, does not earn a dime.

Some great examples of how liberals have established control over states in various areas would be the Department of Education. These department forces states to meet certain standards in their educational systems, taking away from the state the right to decide for themselves. They've created the Environmental Protection Agency to pass laws all states have to abide by in order to protect all things "nature." The Department of Housing and Urban Development provides guidelines to prevent housing discrimination and other protections. There are other examples, but I'm sure you get the point. Where liberals can justify that states are not doing an adequate job in a certain area, they create laws (or new cabinet-level agencies) to move in and take over. Forced bussing is one of those examples. This will be covered a little further into the book.

The result is a bloated bureaucracy that by 2009 was employing more than 2,748,978 people. That's a lot of folks. How much does it cost to pay them and provide a variety of benefits, plus provide all the programs Congress has created to provide for the poor and disadvantaged? During FY 2018, the federal government spent $4.11 trillion, up from a $127 billion or 3.2% vs. FY 2017 spending of $3.99 trillion.

Under the uber-liberal administration of Obama, the national debt grew some 86 percent, from $10.7 trillion to over $21.974 trillion. I've always wondered how allegedly intelligent people could allow our budget to grow far beyond our ability to pay it off. Oh, I forgot—it's not their money. That's why they don't give a damn.

If our household budget were to grow in a similar manner, we'd be forced into a position where bankruptcy would be the only way out. I'm sorry, but to me, this is beyond irresponsible. Why can't our government learn to live within the income/budget that keeps our country solvent? Why do they raise the debt ceiling when they're in need of more money? That's as stupid as coming home and finding your toilets have backed up and the house is full of crap. If you're a liberal politician, you say, "Let's raise the roof in order to make more room for the crap." I guess there truly is no cure for stupid.

Today, we have new members of Congress like Alexandria Ocacio-Cortez (AOC, who I've previously mentioned) wants to provide all the previously mentioned free health care and education for all. The cost for this is estimated to be well over thirty trillion dollars. Under her newly announced Green Plan, she wants a job and salary for everyone, even if the person doesn't want to work. She wants to refurbish *every* building in American so they're all more energy efficient. She wants to create a modern train system so we can do away with air travel and most cars because they all emit too many carbons. Oh, I forgot to mention she also said the world was going to end in twelve years because of global warming.

Where liberals and nonbelievers worry about the world coming to an end, Christians don't. What we have that they lack is hope and faith. The Bible, in Revelations, talks about the end of the world, describes different types of disaster that nature will bring about. This will be the beginning of the final days. This is the Second Coming all Christians await. Those on the left and many on the right who have no faith, or have lost it, fear the predictions put out by the wacky global warning extremists. The faith we have in our Heavenly Father and the predictions in the Bible sustains us. Our faith and hope in one day joining our Savior gives us strength to continue living and moving forward. Not cowering in some corner crying the sky is falling like so many "chicken little's" today.

AOC also wants to close prisons and do away with Immigration and Customs Enforcement (ICE). If you're a clear-thinking American (who has lived longer than three decades and done more with their life than tend bar or wait on tables in restaurants) wondering what fantasyland she and the rest of her ilk are living in, join the club. They give no thought to where those prisoners now incarcerated will go. Who will continue the enforcement work current ICE personnel is performing? These are the rantings of pie-eyed dreamers whose education has clearly failed them, as has life in general. Don't forget to check out the Green program she's pushing that I mentioned.

There are also border security and immigration issues that really show us where the left stands when it comes to protecting this country and its people. The left wants open borders, and sadly, that includes some Republicans. They support sanctuary cities and states. They don't want the police (ICE) being allowed to take custody of illegal immigrant criminals once released from jails. They make light of the numerous examples of American citizens killed at the hands of these illegals, thus again demonstrating that they care more for these criminals than they do for the people who are legitimate members of our communities.

This was again on display during two recent democratic debates, each with ten of the presidential hopefuls attending. When ask if they'd give up their health care (congress has a very good one compared to most Americans) only three of four raised their hands. This is very telling because it falls in line with the left's normal mode of business when passing laws. They pass laws we must follow while exempting them. During this same two days of debate they were ask who among them would give illegal's free health care. Virtually all of them raised their hands. There is no doubt in my mind these so called representatives of our country and society care more for people who are not citizens and here illegally. They pay lip service to the homeless and those without health care while making little to no effort to fix the problems for our own country men and women.

What also came out during these debates was the issue of forced bussing that took place during the sixties and seventies. Why bring that up? Are some of these people thinking about resurrecting that terrible program again? Really?

In 1954, the U.S. Supreme Court landmark decision in *Brown v. Board of Education* declared racial segregation in public schools unconstitutional. The process of integrating public schools met fierce resistance in the South where segregation laws took hold after the American Civil War and the Reconstruction era of the United States. In Northern and Western states, *de facto* segregation was the customary practice. Due to patterns of residential segregation, a principal tool for racial integration was the use of busing. In the 1971 *Swann v. Charlotte-Mecklenburg Board of Education* ruling, the Supreme Court ruled that the federal courts had the discretion to include busing as a desegregation tool to achieve racial balance. While the *Swann* decision addressed *de jure* segregation in the South, it failed to address *de facto* segregation which persisted elsewhere in the country. In Georgia, Governor Jimmy Carter saw that *Swann* was "clearly a one-sided decision; the Court is still talking about the South, the North is still going free". In the 1974 *Milliken v. Bradley* decision, the U.S. Supreme Court placed an important limitation on *Swann* when they ruled that students could be bused across district lines only when evidence of *de jure* segregation across multiple school districts existed.

In the 1970s and 1980s, under federal court supervision, many school districts implemented mandatory busing plans within their district. A few of these plans are still in use today. An example of stiff resistance to desegregation busing was the Restore Our Alienated Rights movement in Boston.

Since the 1980s, desegregation busing has been in decline. Even though school districts provided zero-fare bus transportation to and from for students' assigned schools, those schools were in some cases many miles away from students' homes, which often presented problems to them and their families. In addition, many families were angry about having to send their children miles to another school in an unfamiliar neighborhood when there was an available school a short distance away. The movement of large numbers of white families to suburbs of large cities, so-called white flight, reduced the effectiveness of the policy. Many whites who stayed moved their children into private or parochial schools; these effects combined to make many urban school districts predominantly nonwhite, reducing any effectiveness mandatory busing may have had. In addition, school districts started using magnet schools, new school construction, and more detailed computer-generated information to refine their school assignment plans.

Due to these efforts and the fact that housing patterns had changed, by the early 1990s, most school districts had been released from court supervision and ceased using mandatory busing to try to desegregate schools. However, many continued to provide a similar level of school bus services, because families had become accustomed to the transportation and to the school choice available in recent assignment programs. (The above explanation was taken from the American History USA website entitled bussing.)

Try and imagine the anger and frustration families from coast to coast experienced. In the majority of cases these were families who had moved to a city or neighborhoods where the school system was considered excellent. This was for the benefit of getting the best education for their children possible. Then, because of court decisions, liberal politicians tell you your child will not be attending that school, but instead will be bused to a school miles away from his home in order to acquire equality. And the school they might be going to was not in a good neighborhood or that good of a school system. I mentioned earlier watching TV when I was in school in the sixties when the Governor of Alabama stood on the Montgomery city high school steps personally blocking the entrance of blacks into the all white school.

You must also keep in mind that our congress was controlled by the democrats for more than forty years. During that time they also had control of the White House for much of it. In a word, they controlled everything and were able to enforce their will on the whole country. Over the years this same desire to control has gotten stronger with these people.

It wasn't until the 1994 midterm elections during Clinton's first term that republicans regained control of the House of Representatives. Newt Gingrich was elected Speaker of the House and introduced the "Contract with America." The following are the contents of that contract. They reflect the direction and honesty (then) republicans wanted to the government to take. Democrats hated it because it laid bear their dishonest and deceitful nature. It shined the light on how they had been running things in Washington DC for the previous four decades.

The Contract with America was the conservative action of more than 300 Republican Congressional candidates who signed it. Led by the Speaker of the House Newt Gingrich, the contract was presented at a September 27, 1994 press conference.

The following is a proposal, as well as the actual contract that was presented by Republican Members of the House of Representatives.

The Contract with America is rooted in three core principles:

Accountability. The government is too big and spends too much, and Congress and unelected bureaucrats have become so entrenched to be unresponsive to the public they are supposed to serve. The GOP contract restores accountability to government.

Responsibility. Bigger government and more federal programs usurp personal responsibility from families and individuals. The GOP contract restores a proper balance between government and personal responsibility.

Opportunity. The American Dream is out of the reach of too many families because of burdensome government regulations and harsh tax laws. The GOP contract restores the American dream.

The Contract

As Republican Members of the House of Representatives and as citizens seeking to join that body we propose not just to change its policies, but even more important, to restore the bonds of trust between the people and their elected representatives. That is why, in this era of official evasion and posturing, we offer instead a detailed agenda for national renewal, a written commitment with no fine print.

This year's election offers the chance, after four decades of one-party control, to bring to the House a new majority that will transform the way Congress works. That historic change would be the end of government that is too big, too intrusive, and too easy with the public's money. It can be the beginning of a Congress that respects the values and shares the faith of the American family. Like Lincoln, our first Republican president, we intend to act "with firmness in the right, as God gives us to see the right." To restore accountability to Congress. To end its cycle of scandal and disgrace. To make us all proud again of the way free people govern themselves.

On the first day of the 104th Congress, the new Republican majority will immediately pass the following major reforms, aimed at restoring the faith and trust of the American people in their government:

First: Require all laws that apply to the rest of the country also apply equally to the Congress. (Up to that point democrats passed laws on the rest of the country, but exempted themselves.)

Second: Select a major, independent auditing firm to conduct a comprehensive audit of Congress for waste, fraud or abuse.

Third: Cut the number of House committees, and cut committee staff by one-third.

Fourth: Limit the terms of all committee chairs.

Fifth: Ban the casting of proxy votes in committee.

Sixth: Require committee meetings to be open to the public.

Seventh: Require a three-fifths majority vote to pass a tax increase.

Eighth: Guarantee an honest accounting of our Federal Budget by implementing zero base-line budgeting. (Force the government to live within its budget like any normal household had too.)

Thereafter, within the first 100 days of the 104th Congress, we shall bring to the House Floor the following bills, each to be given full and open debate, each to be given a clear and fair vote and each to be immediately available this day for public inspection and scrutiny.

1. **The Fiscal Responsibility Act;** A balanced budget/tax limitation amendment and a legislative line-item veto to restore fiscal responsibility to an out-of-control Congress, requiring them to live under the same budget constraints as families and businesses. (Republicans had been trying to pass a line-item veto law for the president. This would have allowed him to veto certain parts of spending bills without killing the whole bill. Democrats always fought this because they like to add additional spending items to a bill, referred to as "pork."
2. **The Taking Back Our Streets Act;** An anti-crime package including stronger truth-in-sentencing, "good faith" exclusionary rule exemptions, effective death penalty provisions,

and cuts in social spending from this summer's "crime" bill to fund prison construction and additional law enforcement to keep people secure in their neighborhoods and kids safe in their schools.

3. **The Personal Responsibility Act;** Discourage illegitimacy and teen pregnancy by prohibiting welfare to minor mothers and denying increased AFDC for additional children while on welfare, cut spending for welfare programs, and enact a tough two-years-and-out provision with work requirements to promote individual responsibility.

4. **The Family Reinforcement Act;** Child support enforcement, tax incentives for adoption, strengthening rights of parents in their children's education, stronger child pornography laws, and an elderly dependent care tax credit to reinforce the central role of families in American society.

5. **The American Dream Restoration Act;** A S500 per child tax credit, begin repeal of the marriage tax penalty, and creation of American Dream Savings Accounts to provide middle class tax relief.

6. **The National Security Restoration Act;** No U.S. troops under U.N. command and restoration of the essential parts of our national security funding to strengthen our national defense and maintain our credibility around the world.

7. **The Senior Citizens' Fairness Act;** Raise the Social Security earnings limit which currently forces seniors out of the work force, repeal the 1993 tax hikes on Social Security benefits and provide tax incentives for private long-term care insurance to let Older Americans keep more of what they have earned over the years.

8. **The Job Creation and Wage Enhancement Act;** Small business incentives, capital gains cut and indexation, neutral cost recovery, risk assessment/cost-benefit analysis, strengthening the Regulatory Flexibility Act and unfunded mandate reform to create jobs and raise worker wages.

9. **The Common Sense Legal Reform Act;** "Loser pays" laws, reasonable limits on punitive damages and reform of

product liability laws to stem the endless tide of litigation. (This was fought tooth and nail by lawyers. It would have probably cut by seventy-five percent the number of law suits they would have been able to file, thus hitting them directly in their collective pocket books.)

10. **The Citizen Legislature Act;** A first-ever vote on term limits to replace career politicians with citizen legislators. (No democrat, and a good number of republicans, has ever wanted this to happen. They want to be able to continue in office for as long as they like. The power is intoxicating.)

Further, we will instruct the House Budget Committee to report to the floor and we will work to enact additional budget savings, beyond the budget cuts specifically included in the legislation described above, to ensure that the Federal budget deficit will be less than it would have been without the enactment of these bills. (This information can be found on the United States History website.)

For me, it's clear. Democrats have always conducted themselves and their activities in a manner as to look legitimate, but in reality to be unscrupulous and under handed. That's why they want more uneducated, poor immigrants in this country who will eventually become voters and help keep them in power. It's just that simple.

It's also clear the majority of Americans don't want people telling them how to live, what they can and cannot eat (someone should tell Corey Booker who wants to limit the amount of red meat we eat, or De Blasio, New York's mayor who thinks 32 oz drinks are way too big). Telling others how to live, what not to eat, and other controlling measures are also the main faults of liberalism. They have no clue how to just leave people alone to live the lives the way they deem fit. Why do the folks on the left feel this driving need to tell the rest of us what is and is not good for us? Yet when someone on the right complains about their drug use and promiscuous sexual conduct, they're the ones crying about being left alone to do their thing without criticism. This is referred to as moral relativism by these sinners.

It's also telling when the president threatens to send illegal aliens to sanctuary cities, who actively protect illegal from immigration authorities, only to accuse the president of acting illegally and immorally. Their reaction has again shown us their double standard and hypocrisy. They don't mind breaking the law by shielding illegal aliens and criminals, but when the president says he's going to send them more, they protest. Really?

It should be noted that Article VI of our Constitution establishes the Supremacy Clause. This clause tells us that all the Constitution and the laws of the United States are to be the supreme law of the land. This means the states may not pass any laws or disobey federal laws as this is a violation of this article.

So I ask you. How is it that marijuana has been legalized in a number of states but is still against the federal statues? Or take into consideration the state of California and various other cities from coast to coast who have passed laws or ordinances allowing the protection of illegal aliens. These so-called sanctuary places are in complete violation of federal law. This is yet another example of the double standard liberals chose to follow. They'll obey only those laws they like and ignore the ones they don't. wow! I'm still waiting for the feds to take these cities and California to federal court in order to prosecute them for these glaring violations.

Today's Political Quagmire

When Donald Trump was running in the primaries, he was not my choice for president. When he won the Republican nomination, he got my support. He was clearly the lesser of two evils.

What I've come to see about Trump is he doesn't change. His attitude about key issues remains the same the first time he airs it, and later after commentary and discussion by the media pundits and others. It's always the same. Also true about his personality. Unlike virtually every democrat whose views change depending with whom they're speaking or which way the wind is blowing. They're like chameleons changing the colors depending on the vegetation (or excrement) they're in. Would I like for Trump to tone down some of his tweets and commentary about the media and his opposition? Not really. I like finally having a conservative who doesn't tuck his tail between his legs when the media and leftist members of congress attack him. He strikes back.

Hillary Clinton, along with her husband, Slick Willy, had and have demonstrated for several decades that they are both liars and crooks. Both are completely dishonest right down to their bone marrow. Between the two of them, Madam Hillary is the most power-hungry. These two don't give a damn about this country and its people. They care only for how much richer they can get and how much more power they can wield. I remember someone asking a colleague of mine how do you know when Bill or Hillary are lying.

His response was, "their mouths are moving." This has been well documented by several books. Here are a just a few:

Hell to Pay by Barbra Olson

The Final Days by Barbra Olson

Absolute Power by David Limbaugh

Hillary's Scheme by Carl Limbaucher Jr.

Madam Hillary by E. Tyrrell Jr.

Rewriting History by Dick Morris

Because He Could by Dick Morris

Unlimited Access by Gary Aldrich

The Extreme Makeover of Hillary Clinton by Buchanan Bay

The Vast Right-Wing Conspiracy's Dossier on Hillary Clinton by Amanda B Carpenter

Legacy: Paying the Price for the Clinton Years by Rich Lowry

Shattered: Inside Hillary Clinton's Doomed Campaign by Johnathan Allen and Amie Parnes

Crisis of Character by Gary Bryne

You can go to Amazon to read the descriptions of each book in order to understand the direction each author is taking. For instance, Gary Aldrich was one of two FBI agents assigned to the White House. He started under George H. W. Bush and was there for the transition when Clinton won the presidency. His description of the complete difference in decorum and moral conduct between the two families and the people they brought into the White House is truly eye-opening. One key example was the Bush White House had a traditional Christmas tree with the kinds of ornaments one would expect. The Clinton's tree had things you would definitely not expect, like condoms hanging from the branches. For me, that spoke volumes about the Clintons and the mind-set they and their ilk have about Christ's birthday. You can check out others to learn more. Dick Morris was the Clinton's political advisor. He helped Bill win the 1992 election and the 1996 election before having a falling out with Hillary. His insights and knowledge about these people are very accurate and stunning.

When Trump won the election, the left was in shock. Virtually, everyone on the left and in the media thought Hillary was a shoo-in. The utter disbelief was clear to anyone who watched the voter results that night as they played out on the various media programs. The leftist pundits and so-called TV personalities were beside themselves with grief and forlorn. You would have thought the world was coming to an end. Of course, for them, it had.

I had to laugh. Watching all these alleged adults act like spoiled middle schoolers who'd just lost their favorite pet was telling. Just like when George W. Bush beat Al Gore in the 2000 presidential race, the left started saying the Electoral College was outdated and obsolete. When the left loses, they look for someone or something to blame. In both cases (Bush and Trump), the left did well in the popular vote but failed to garner the required electoral votes. They never want to accept that their ideologies and liberal desires to create and control a big government machine is not what average Americans are interested in. They are also ignorant about why the founders created the Electoral College in the first place. This is just another example of the failure of the liberal educational system in this country.

What was also telling was the reaction of some in the Republican Party who clearly did not then, nor do they today, like Trump. These people were tagged as the never-Trumpers (this included those on the left). Jeff Flake, Paul Ryan and John McCain are the first ones who come to mind on the Republican side of the aisle. There were a lot more who gave up their seats in congress because they didn't want to work with Trump. Prior to Trump's election win, the mainstream media had tried throwing every kind of imaginary dirt at him they could. They failed miserably.

After the election, they went into overdrive working with the Democrats and their supporters to manufacture allegations of collusion between Trump and the Russians. Until this process started to unfold, I had not seen what Trump and others were describing as the "swamp" in DC, also referred to as the "deep state." This refers to a deeply entrenched hard-core leftist who work below the surface to undermine any conservative that gets elected to the office of the president. Trump's election as president drove them over the edge. Some have even referred to this group as a fifth element.

This resulted in facts and information ultimately coming into the light of day that clearly implicates senior members of the Justice Department (DOJ) and the Federal Bureau of Investigations (FBI) and the late Senator John McCain in colluding with the Clintons to destroy Trump in any way possible. It was discovered that the Clintons had paid for Robert Steele, a former British spy, to manufacture a dossier that indicated Trump had colluded with the Russians to steal the 2016 election from Hillary.

Recent discoveries have shown McCain's involvement in having the dossier passed around was because of the late senator's hatred of Donald Trump. This was because of the presidents criticizing Senator John McCain, saying, "He's not a war hero. He's a war hero because he was captured. I like people that weren't captured." When the Republican-controlled congress voted on repealing and replacing Obama care, McCain was the last member called. When he stood up, he gave the now-famous thumbs down to the measure. A clear "in your face" gesture to Trump. For McCain, it was about getting even. It was vengeful and vindictive retribution against Trump. The concerns of our country and the well-being of health care in American was the least of McCain's concerns. It was revenge.

I was never much of a fan of the late senator. I did and do respect his service and sacrifice for our country. Unlike the president, I understand the reasons behind military personnel becoming prisoners of war. This isn't something anyone does intentionally. How McCain conducted himself, in the end, was very childish and undeserving of someone who had served in the military with such distinction.

As previous discussed, the investigation by Robert Mueller, the former head of the FBI appointed as a special counsel, and a Senate committee for nearly the same time frame, no evidence has been found. When the Republicans controlled the House of Representatives prior to the 2018 midterm elections, they subpoenaed an assortment of documents that alleged those in Congress had been involved in this dossier effort to ruin Trump. The Democrats have yet to release any of those documents. What are they hiding?

Throughout this whole sordid affair, the mainstream media has helped the Democrats cover up the lies and the clear manufacture of allegations in the dossier. They have made no attempt at trying to be neutral and honest in their so-called journalistic reporting. Such is their hatred for Donald Trump. Why haven't more Americans ask the hard questions of the media regarding their dishonest and unprofessional conduct? Why haven't these phonies been kicked to the curb for their lies and complete dishonesty? They are America's state media working hand in glove with the Democrats.

What's truly sad is the number of so-called intelligent people who believe and support their lies and dishonesty. These are the Kool-Aid drinkers of the left (a reference to Jim Jones's followers who participated in mass suicide by drinking a cyanide-laced Kool-Aid under his direction; they were brainwashed by Jones to the point they were no longer rational).

For nearly two years (675 days), this charade investigation by Mueller did not find one scintilla of evidence Trump colluded with the Russian in any manner whatsoever. The final report said it clearly. Yet throughout this whole mess, Congressman Adam Schiff has shouted to the rooftops that he has proof of the collusion. He has yet to provide it. I'm still wondering why someone in the House or Senate for that matter, among those on the right hasn't called his hand. They should tell him to put up or shut up. Here again, we see that complete lack of a backbone I spoke of earlier demonstrated all too often by the Republicans. These guys are so afraid they're going to get hammered by the media they're left cowering in corners, hoping they won't be seen.

What has become ever so clear is the collusion that had taken place on the part of the Clintons, James Comey, the Obama justice department and administration, as well as a number of senior officials in both the justice department and the FBI. FISA courts were lied to in order for these people to spy on Americans. The Steele dossier was used to pull the wool over the judges' eyes. To this date, not one judge has called their hand on it or ask for criminal action to be taken against the parties involved. One has to wonder if these allegedly honest judges were in the bag for the Clintons along with the rest of the aforementioned parties.

What was also interesting and enlightening for me was how similar many politicians are. It doesn't make any difference if they're on the right or left side of the aisle. Both Democrats and Republicans believe they are the anointed ones chosen to rule this country. They make promises they never plan on keeping as well as deals with the opposition behind closed doors.

I've always seen Democrats as walking to the beat of the leadership's drums. Whether it's Schumer or Pelosi, who dictate to the rest of their flock what the party line is going to be, somewhat less so with the Republicans. Then the rank and file in the Congress stays in line. Failure to do so can result in the loss of a crucial seat on an important committee, or worse the, party backs someone else when your seat comes up for reelection.

Just ask Joe Lieberman. He didn't play ball and follow the Democratic leadership's agenda. He followed his heart and the will of those who voted him into office—his constituents. The Democratic Party supported another candidate against Lieberman. When he lost the primary, he ran as an independent and won. That was a real "in your face" moment to the leftist leadership who had tried to punish him for not following their orders.

Two recent incidents demonstrate even more of this totalitarian nature that exists in the Democratic Party. Pelosi has said in so many words those in her party in Congress had better get back with the program (meaning get back in line). This is because Ocasio and Ilhan, among other new freshmen Democrats, have been pushing their agenda and been getting a lot of press coverage. And Ocasio-Cortez said she's making a list of those who don't vote with the party. wow!

While the left marches in lockstep, the right is too timid and afraid to do or say anything that will result in the media and the left jumping them with bad press. As a former Republican, this conduct made me sick. Clearly, too many on the right have not learned the lessons about dealing with the Democrats. It's always their way or the highway. Without question, some on the right are too naïve to understand this, or they just don't care as long as they're left alone. They are gutless and not worth voting for. Another reason for term limits.

Since Trump became president, our country's economy has been reinvigorated. Of course, you won't know anything about this because the vast majority in the media has been keeping it quiet, with the exception of Fox News. The Dems and the media want to keep Trump's successes under wraps, hidden from those who only listen to their fake news buddies. They suppress, denigrate, and outright lie about the status of unemployment, job growth, stifling regulation reductions, and a host of other positive examples that have taken place over the first two years of the Trump's administration. That's just how much they hate this guy. wow!

Now the left is really worried. They've tried for more than two years to destroy Trump in every way possible. They have failed time and time again. The Democrats are worried too many Americans really see the improvements that have taken place under the Trump administration. They heard the doom and gloom Obama laid out regarding the sour economy. Obama said we would not see any more manufacturing jobs returning to our shores. Income would not improve. This list he predicted has all fallen apart. All the things Obama said that wouldn't return have, and with a huge jump in employment, job creations, middle-class income increases, and so on. These facts are what scare the Dems as we get closer to the 2020 elections.

What should also concern them is their conduct and the conduct of their collaborators in the media. The constant nonstop negative news and misrepresentations for the past two years have worn the majority of Americans down. Every time the media or the Democrats say Trump is guilty of this or that, a few days later, they're proven wrong. Their collective track record in this area is astounding.

Now that the Mueller report is out, the Democrats are trying to make a silk purse out of a sow's ear. Jerry Nadler, current chair of the House Judiciary Committee, wants to spin information regarding alleged obstruction of justice from the report into something

Democrats can use to start impeachment proceedings. I hope they do. This will continue to show the American people how stupid and delusional the Democrats have become over their obsession with removing Trump from office. A very recent example was Democrats have taken "God" out of the oath process. They are systematically trying to remove religion in this manner. I don't care what their excuses are, our country and its government have been an organization based on Godly principles. People have been sworn into office and taken oaths in this manner. Now "demoncrats" are stripping the use of God from these processes. What's next?

As I've said, they don't care about the election results. They want to completely overturn the 2016 election results. They don't care about the will of the people or the process established long ago by the founding fathers. They want to rewrite the rules and change the process so they will always win. Elitist snobs and spoiled brats don't even come close to describing who these people really are. Wait until they see the 2020 election results.

Now, assuming the Republicans do keep the White House and retake the House, will it matter? The two previous times they've had a united government (George W. Bush and Trump's first two years where they controlled the government), they didn't eliminate Obamacare (Trump), they didn't fix the immigration laws and problems (Bush and Trump), and they didn't build the wall (Bush and Trump), to name a few of the things they could have done.

In both cases, they wasted the opportunities they had. So why should any of us believe they'll do anything different if they're in control again? In my mind, they're not much better than the Democrats. They demonstrate an elitist mentality. Many of them (Flake, McCain, Paul, and others) have worked against Trump when they could have been helping make our country better. They don't deserve our support.

The Abortion and Death Penalty Issues

Abortion

To discuss this issue is to inflame emotions on both sides. There's the prochoice group who now demand abortions even during and shortly after the delivery of a full-term baby. There's the prolife side that holds all life as sacred. As a person who was adopted at two months of age, I'm clearly prolife. As a Christian, I cannot understand how one human being could be okay with killing a child, at any stage.

The New York State Legislature recently passed a law allowing abortion at birth. AT BIRTH!! After Governor Cuomo signed the bill, the chamber erupted into applause. The governor of Virginia, Ralph Northam, a medical doctor, also suborns this horrid conduct. He is okay with infanticide, which clearly violates his Hippocratic Oath. During a TV interview, he tried explaining how a child could be delivered, and then a discussion between the doctor and the mother would take place regarding her desire to keep or terminate the child. These people are clearly Godless and immoral. They are the face of the Democratic Party today.

A bill was introduced in the Senate that would protect babies delivered alive. Democrats argued that this violated a woman's reproductive rights. Forty-four Democrats voted against the bill. These men and women, regardless of their arguments, are totally comfortable with killing a child after birth if the mother doesn't want it. For

Democrats, the rights and life of a baby depend only on whether the mother wants it or not. To them, the life of a baby is meaningless and secondary to the desires of the mother. For me these people have no soul. They have no moral compass. They are devoid of emotions, empathy and a sense of caring for the babies who are incapable of protecting themselves.

These politicians and their followers have clearly shown us who they are and where they stand when it comes to the life of an unborn or newly born baby. It's a life of no consequence to these heartless and morally bankrupt people. Most of the women who support the murder of these children do so for selfish reasons. Their reproductive rights trump the life and well-being of any child they may be responsible for bringing into the world.

A bill was passed and signed into law by the governor of Georgia that makes abortion illegal once a fetal heartbeat is detected. The liberal "abortion at any time" crowd has gone crazy. Two Hollywood filmmakers, David Simon and Christine Vachon, have vowed to not work in the state again. For them, like their liberal buddies on the left coast, the woman and her desires are more important than a baby's life. Looks like I'll have to start paying attention to who the filmmakers are from now on so as not to support anything people like Simon and Vachon.

Likewise activist and actress Alyssa Milano called for a "sex strike." That's right. She's asking her followers to protest by not having sex until "we get bodily autonomy back." That's where her mind and morals are located. When I googled her to find out the exact words of her challenge to her fans I found several porn links she's featured in. Had no idea she was a porn star. Go figure.

This is the face of liberalism today. Any woman who can agree with such a procedure cannot be a person who truly believes in God. They are utterly devoid of a moral compass. This is the time, from their conception to when these little human beings are old enough to survive outside of their mother, where these babies are helpless and at the mercy of the woman who conceived them.

Based on the latest data from states, approximately 879,000 abortions took place in the United States in 2017. This was down from approximately 892,000 abortions in 2016 and 913,000 abortions in 2015. This takes place each year. I cringe when I think of the millions of babies who were never given a chance at life because of some selfish, self-centered woman who didn't want the responsibility.

I give thanks to God that I was born at a time when abortion was not nearly as prevalent and popular as it is today. I was given the opportunity to live a wonderful life, meet and marry my soul mate, have two beautiful intelligent daughters who have given us beautiful grandbabies. Had my natural mother chosen abortion, I would have been denied all of that. No one has the right to make that decision for another person. No one has the right to play God with another life.

Dana Loesch captures not only the horrid practice of killing babies in her book, *Fly Over Nation*; she also chronicles the topic of euthanasia, the practice of doctor-assisted suicide. In this latter topic, the left claims it's about a person's dignity and right to die whenever they choose. In either case, it highlights the complete lack of any knowledge or faith in God in these people's lives. There are Bible verses that speak to this very issue.

> *1 Corinthians 3:17: "If any man defile the temple of God, him shall God destroy; for the temple of God is holy, which [temple] ye are."*
>
> *1 Corinthians 6:19–20: "Know ye not that your body is the temple of the Holy Ghost [which is] in you, which ye have of God, and ye are not your own?"*
>
> *Ecclesiastes 7:17: "Be not over much wicked, neither be thou foolish: why shouldest thou die before thy time?"*

The Planned Parenthood movement was started by Margret Sanger. *Wikipedia* describes Margaret Higgins Sanger was an American birth control activist, sex educator, writer, and nurse. Sanger popularized the term *birth control*, opened the first birth control clinic in the United States, and established organizations that evolved into the Planned Parenthood Federation of America.

Those of us who have studied her, we know her to be is a cold-blooded racist. Sanger believed in the concept of eugenics. The dictionary describes *eugenics* as the science of improving a human population by controlled breeding to increase the occurrence of desirable heritable characteristics. Developed largely by Francis Galton as a method of improving the human race, it fell into disfavor only after the perversion of its doctrines by the Nazis.

Hitler wanted to create a super race of perfect humans. Eugenics, or selective breeding, was the vehicle he used. Sanger wanted to eliminate those she saw as inferior. Here are some of her beliefs, in her own words as found published by Diane S. Dew (www.dianedew. com).

The Roots of Birth Control from the Woman Who Created It

On blacks, immigrants, and indigents:

> *"'Human weeds,' 'reckless breeders,' spawning human beings who never should have been born,"* Margret Sanger, *Pivot of Civilization* (referring to immigrants and poor people).

On sterilization and racial purification:

> *"Sanger believed that, for the purpose of "purification," couples should be rewarded who chose sterilization"* Birth Control in America: The Career of Margret Sanger, by David Kennedy (p. 117, quoting a 1923 Sanger speech).

On the right of married couples to bear children:

> *"Couples should be required to submit applications to have a child, she wrote in her 'Plan for Peach'"* Birth Control Review, April 1932.

On the purpose of birth control:

"The purpose in promoting birth control was "to create a race of thoroughbreds," she wrote in the *Birth Control Review*, Nov. 1921.

On the rights of the handicapped and mentally ill, and racial minorities:

"More children from the fit, less from the unfit—that is the chief aim of birth control" Birth Control Review, May 1919, p. 12.

On the extermination of blacks:

"We do not want word to go out that we want to exterminate the Negro population," she said, "if ever occurs to any of their more rebellious members," *Woman's Body, Woman's Right: A Social History of Birth Control in America,* by Linda Gordon.

On respecting the rights of the mentally ill:

"In her 'Plan for Peace,' Sanger outlined her strategy for eradication of those she deemed 'feebleminded.' Among the steps included in her evil scheme were immigration restrictions; compulsory sterilization; segregation to a lifetime of farm work; etc." *Birth Control Review*, April 1932, p.107.

These are just a few of her quotes. You can easily Google others if you wish to learn more. After reading these, you should have no illusions about why Planned Parenthood was created. While I find it hard to believe all prochoice women believe what Sanger stood for, one must ask the question of how deep into the well have they fallen.

The Bible is very clear on the issue of abortion. In addition to the sixth commandment, telling us, "Thou shalt not murder," we also find a more specific reference to the unborn in Exodus 21:22, which is the first fetal homicide law and concerns the child harmed during a separate assault. Pro-abortion theologians wrongly interpret this passage to refer to miscarriage, and only if the woman also dies is the penalty then life for life.

But the passage distinguishes between the baby who survives the assault and the baby who dies. The meaning turns on whether the woman has a miscarriage or gives birth prematurely. And the Hebrew verb used is *not* that for miscarriage. Therefore the passage imposes only a fine on the criminal who accidentally causes premature birth, but the punishment is life for life if the baby then dies. This shows that God equated the life of the unborn with that of the born, and abortion with murder.

I understand this will evoke a great deal of backlash and resent-ment. Tough! That's life. Life is precious and should be protected. Clearly, something liberals have difficulty understanding, depend-ing on whether you're talking about the unborn to be terminated or the sociopathic criminal who's guilty of heinous murder and other unspeakable crimes. Liberals would rather keep these animals alive and terminate the innocent. Go figure.

When I taught my college students about this subject, they were given an assignment to research Margret Sanger. They were provided a list of questions to answer. When the assignment was due, I asked the students what their thoughts and impressions were. Virtually every student was astounded that this woman was the founder of Planned Parenthood. Some told me they had difficulty getting their head around the fact that Sanger encouraged eliminating babies because they were from inferior people. I explained to them that this is a key problem with our society. Too many ignorant people. These important lessons are not being taught by leftist teachers because they don't want the truth to be known. It flies in the face of the pro-choice movement.

I've often wondered why more people don't take the time and make the effort to become more knowledgeable about the issues and the players. Instead, they buy the lies and propaganda the left-wing media is constantly selling. The ignorant and the unwashed of our society; they serve the Democrats well.

The Death Penalty

Now, what I find really funny about these prochoice people is their stance on the death penalty. Many of them are against sending a person to death row for any reason, even after the proper due process within legal system has run its course. They have absolutely no problem with trying to keep a cold-blooded sociopath alive while not even blinking an eye at killing a fetus, or now a newborn.

Clearly, these are people who have never had to deal with one of these emotionless sociopathic killers. Anyone who has spent any time around the penal system knows there are hundreds across the country who are a danger to society. Many are kept in solitary confinement twenty-three hours a day because they are too dangerous to be left in the general population. They serve no purpose, and society derives no benefit from keeping them alive. These are the kinds of people AOC would release if she were to get her way regarding closing prisons. Clearly, the comments of a person who has no idea what she would put into motion if that were to occur.

There are also Bible passages that speak directly to this issue. Here are a few from the Old Testament for your review and contemplation.

1. *Exodus 21:12: "He that smiteth a man, so that he die, shall be surely put to death."*
2. *Numbers 35:16–17: "But if someone strikes and kills another person with a piece of iron, it is murder, and the murderer must be executed. Or if someone with a stone in his hand*

strikes and kills another person, it is murder, and the murderer must be put to death."

3. *Deuteronomy 19:11–12: "But if out of hate someone lies in wait, assaults and kills a neighbor, and then flees to one of these cities, the killer shall be sent for by the town elders, be brought back from the city, and be handed over to the avenger of blood to die."*

4. *Exodus 21:14–17 "But if a man come presumptuously upon his neighbour, to slay him with guile; thou shalt take him from mine altar, that he may die. And he that smiteth his father, or his mother, shall be surely put to death. And* he that stealeth a man, *and selleth him, or if he be found in his hand, he shall surely be put to death. And* he that curseth his father, *or his mother, shall surely be put to death."*

5. *Deuteronomy 27:24 "Cursed is anyone who kills their neighbor secretly." Then all the people shall say, "Amen!"*

6. *Numbers 35:30–32: "Anyone who kills a person is to be put to death as a murderer only on* the testimony *of witnesses. But no one is to be put to death on the testimony of only one witness. Do not accept a ransom for the life of a murderer, who deserves to die. They are to be put to death. Do not accept a ransom for anyone who has fled to a city of refuge and so allow them to go back and live on their own land before the death of the high priest."*

7. *Genesis 9:6: "If anyone takes a human life, that person's life will also be taken by human hands. For God made human beings in his own image."*

It doesn't take much time reviewing the cases of men and women who were adjudicated and sentenced to death to understand why the law exists. The heinous nature of the crimes many of these sociopaths committed in taking a life (or lives) is truly disturbing. I said early at the beginning in the introduction, I believe the military and police are the sheepdogs of society. While the military protects us from threats outside our borders, police put their lives on the line throughout our states and cities.

Police officers strive to protect average citizens from the wolves who would give no thought to killing them and their families. That's why I said in the intro, I believe in both national and personal defense. I refuse to allow some animal to hurt or abuse my family. As long as God gives me a clear mind and the physical ability to respond, they will be dealt with. If you can't find it in your heart to do the same for your loved ones, God help you. There will come a time when you will regret not having undergone the training and preparations needed to protect those you love. If you use the excuse that "that happens to other people," you're suffering from cranial anal inversion.

Over the years of working for the sheriff department and taking convicted felons to prison, coupled with the documentaries that clearly show how dangerous and demented some of these inmates are, I've come to believe a large number of them are no different than a mad, ravenous dog and should be dealt with accordingly. When gang leaders who are incarcerated can decree a death sentence for someone outside of prison, let alone another prisoner, one has to wonder why these people are allowed to continue their existence. They provide no service or benefit to society. They use up food and resources that could be used for productive men and women, the homeless, and poor.

I know you might be asking how can I say that and still profess to be a Christian. If we truly followed God's laws, these people would have been put to death. Yet we have a society that believes in forgiveness and allowing people to get a second chance. Just look at the conviction records of these people and what they've done even while in prison, then think again. Those who are driven strictly by their emotions (liberals) fail to see, let alone understand, the realities of this world. These are the people who will be the first to die if the rule of law is allowed to disappear and chaos and anarchy to prevail. Like the cliché about walking a mile in my shoes goes, you cannot understand because you have not walked the trail I've walked.

Politicians, Their Honesty and Moral Compass

(Or Lack Of)

When I look back on how politicians have conducted themselves, I think of Ted Kennedy who allowed his date (even though he was married), Mary Jo Kopechne, on the night of July 18, 1969, to drown in a car he drove into the waters of the Chappaquiddick. His side of the story was he tried several times to save her, diving repeatedly into the waters. Whether that is true or not, no one really knows. What is known is he didn't report the accident to the police until ten o'clock the following morning. Why, you ask, did he wait so long? In my forty-six years of experience as a veteran of law enforcement, I believe he was drunk and didn't want to be arrested. He had presidential aspirations and didn't want to jeopardize that. His family's allies went into full disinformation mode, trying every way possible to muddy the waters until the incident became overshadowed by other things in the news. Kennedy made one attempt for the presidency and lost to an unpopular candidate—Jimmy Carter.

Or we can look at former secretary of state John Kerry who was ousted by the Swift Boat crew of the Vietnam era with whom he served as having falsified some of the Purple Heart awards he earned while a member of their crews. This took place during Kerry's 2004 presidential bid. While other crew members served full tours of thirteen months, Kerry only served four. Why? Why did he get special treatment when everyone else was required to serve the full thirteen months? Captain George Elliott, USN retired, wrote the following:

> I served with these guys. I went on missions with them, and these men served honorably. Up and down the chain of command, there was no acquiescence to atrocities. It was not condoned, it did not happen, and it was not reported to me verbally or in writing by any of these men including Lt. (Jg) Kerry.
>
> In 1971, '72, for almost 18 months, he (Kerry) stood before the television audiences and claimed that the 500,000 men and women in Vietnam, and in combat, were all villains—there were no heroes. This was after he threw his medals over the fence of the White House. Was that a political stunt, or a true protest? From my stand point, taking in the whole of the picture, I'd say it was a political side show. It worked because he was elected to the Senate. In 2004, our hero from the Vietnam War is running for President of the United States and Commander-in-Chief. Is this now the nature of those on the left who seek the highest office in the land? False accusations against men and women who served their country honorably? Carnival style side shows for the cameras in order to gain the public's attention. Only history will truly judge this guy for what he is and what he did to gain his prominence in politics.

This commentary by Capt. Elliot was found at Snopes.com. There are others you will find that say the same thing about Kerry, as well as those who were more positive. He was not an honorable man. He was a liar who fabricated false accusations against men and women who served in Vietnam for political purposes. There is no lower snake in the grass than one who will lie and denigrate those who served their country honorably in time of war. Kerry lost his presidential bid because of the publicity put forth by the Swift Boat crew members.

Jimmy Carter became our thirty-ninth president after winning the election in November of 1976. While Carter is seen by many as a giving and charitable person, others see him as the man who gave us Islamic terrorism, born of the Islamic Revolutionary Council of Iran. Carter's foreign policy blunders included giving away the Panama Canal and causing the Iranian Revolution.

In November of 1979, radical students overran the American Embassy, taking sixty-six Americans captive. These citizens were held for 444 days. Carter attempted to put together a rescue that ended disastrously, losing valuable equipment and personnel. This was the result of trying to give various military units a role in the operation instead of keeping it within the special ops community.

It resulted in the monarch of Iran, our ally Mohammad Reza Shah Pahlavi, being ousted by the Grand Ayatollah Ruhollah Khomeini, one of the leaders of the revolutionary movement. While many say Carter may be one of our greatest presidents, the truth is he could not free sixty-six of our citizens from the zealots of Iran. It took Ronald Reagan winning the presidency in 1981 before Iran released our people.

The Iranians did not fear Carter. He was seen as weak and incapable of leading. Reagan, on the other hand, was seen as someone who would not play games with Iran. They blinked, and our people came home. Thanks to Carter, we've had forty years of terrorism bought and paid for by Iran. Iran is seen as the biggest supporter of terrorism in the world, funding the likes of Hezbollah, Hamas, and Al-Qaeda, to mention a few. All this because Carter was consumed with human rights concerns, and in not supporting those countries he believed abused them. How many have been abused and murdered by terror attacks in the past forty years, Jimmy?

The Clintons are in a category all their own. I've already provided a list of books by various authors that provide a hard look at who these two people are and what makes them tick. A check of the

Truth or Fiction web site entitled "Clinton Body Count Rumor" provides a great number of examples where the Clintons were under suspicion or investigation (e.g., Whitewater, Travelgate, the Vince Foster death, the Paula Jones and Monica Lewinsky sex scandals, Filegate, the Benghazi disaster, the Clinton Foundation quid pro quo dealings while she was secretary of State, and the private email server with illegally stored and shared classified documents). There are a surprising number of people who died mysteriously or committed suicide. While no one has been able to come up with links or evidence involving the Clintons, there is a great deal of mystery surrounding them in all these events. For me, the old adage that says, "Where there's smoke, there's fire," comes to mind.

Without a doubt, the Clintons have had a great number of controversies surrounding their political lives compared to any of the political cronies past or present. I urge the reader to visit the website above for additional information. The two areas of controversy that should be highlighted are Hillary's failure to protect Americans during the Benghazi tragedy and the clear efforts to cover up her numerous violations of mishandling classified information. This includes destroying hard drives, burning or shredding classified documents, improper use and storage of classifieds, and so on.

For me, the most egregious failure was Hillary's incompetence in protecting her personnel in Benghazi. As the secretary of State, she was responsible for the safety and protection of Ambassador Stevens and all those stationed in Libya to support him. The radical situation in that country continued getting worse—so much so other countries had closed their embassies or counsels and brought their people home. Clinton and Obama made no effort to send help, nor did they make an honest effort at bringing them home.

On the eleventh anniversary of 9/11, the compound where Stevens was staying was attacked. Throughout the whole incident, there is little to no mention of what was taking place back in DC. Evidently, both Clinton and Obama were in the White House situation room, watching what was transpiring. They could have sent military in to assist, but didn't. Instead, they let Americans die and tried to cover it up with a lie about an anti-Muslim video that had inflamed the radicals in Libya. They had Susan Rice parade herself before numerous media personalities on TV and radio, telling the same lie about the video over and over again. Rice will forever be seen as the chief liar and propagandist for Obama and Hillary during this tragedy.

The movie *13 hours: The Secret Soldiers of Benghazi* provides a close-enough accounting for one to understand what happened. None of these people (Obama, Hillary, and those who might have had the backbone to do something but didn't) have any honor or integrity. Their conduct is clear evidence of their spineless and incompetent handling of foreign policy and in protecting American citizens abroad.

Our buddy Slick Willy also has blood on his hands in the form of the Mogadishu fight that resulted in two Blackhawk helicopters being shot down, eighteen dead, and sixty-three wounded. The military leadership had asked for armor in the form of Abram tanks and Bradley fighting vehicles, only to be denied by Clinton. It seems liberals who never served in the military and have no clue regarding military tactics and strategies would be willing to listen to those who do. Sadly, they don't because of the animus they feel toward the men and women in uniform, regardless of military or civilian. Clearly, Clinton is yet another example of a dishonest politician who has no honor, integrity, or moral compass. Yet people on the left love these guys. What does that say about them?

So we have clear evidence based on failed actions by Carter, Bill and Hillary Clinton, and Obama—that they are incompetent when it comes to handling military tactics and strategy, along with foreign policy. They all but ignore military advice because they don't care for or respect those who wear the uniform of our country. Carter should have had some understanding since he served in the US Navy. These people are gutless politicians who are good at talking but clueless when it comes to taking proper actions. Having so many competent people (in the military and intelligence communities) who can provide good advice and guidance in how to deal with situations that politicians have no background in, and not using them, is stupid.

Now we come to the long time self-proclaimed Socialist of the left—Bernie Sanders. Bernie is the senator from Vermont since 2007. Since day one, he has been the only politician to claim he was a socialist, unlike the rest of leftist democrats who steered clear of the socialism title for years. Sanders has railed against the rich and pushed for free health care, free education, and taxing the rich. When he was younger, he stood in solidarity with Fidel Castro as Cuba was becoming a Communist state. Sanders and other leftists have more in common with Communist leaders than they do with their own country and its freedoms.

Bernie Sander constantly pushes for higher taxes on not only the rich but big corporations. He is a multimillionaire in his own right. He's made over a million on book sales over the past two years. He owns a condo in Washington DC that probably cost close to a million, if not more. He also owns a lake house in Vermont, along with another residence. The lake house is valued at over $700K.

During a recent town hall meeting hosted by Bret Bair and Martha McCallum of Fox News, Sanders was asked why he doesn't send a check to the treasury for the difference since he only paid 26 percent in taxes, and is advocating 52 percent wealth tax. True to the way liberals like to play the game, they tell us one thing, only to do something else. Sanders said he paid what he owed. Then he shot back at McCallum, "Why don't you donate your salary?" McCallum responded, saying she wasn't the one who proposed the 52 percent wealth tax. Trying to deflect the criticism by throwing someone else into the picture is a common tactic used by politicians, especially on the left.

Bernie is another example of liberal politicians who like to tell you, "Do as I say, not as I do." They are not people who lead by example. They want to impose taxes and rules on us while they quietly exempt themselves. They are without a doubt the biggest group of liars and con artists in our country. They are hypocrites of the first order. About the only response I have for dealing with them is to pass term limits.

Then there's our first black president. There was so much hope and expectations this guy would set things right in our country because of the nonstop guilt complex many liberal whites have over our country's past history with slavery. This is interesting to me because it was our liberal friends, the Democrats, who supported slavery and were instrumental in bringing about the Civil War. Abraham Lincoln's election to the White House seems to be the proverbial straw that started things in motion in April of 1861.

Over the years, Democrats have fought to keep blacks under their collective boots by means of a "poll tax," property ownership, and other such Jim Crow laws. Even up until the 1964 Civil Rights Act and the 1965 Voting Rights Act, you'll find the Democrats voting against giving these important protections to the black community. Yet today, most blacks think it's the Democrats who have their backs. Just goes to show you how the histories of these events have been lost or rewritten by the left. Because people don't study and learn from history, they are condemned to repeat it.

What's truly sad about the Obama presidency is what he gave us. Once in office, he went touring to different countries, apologizing for the perceived arrogance and bad conduct of the USA. He and Pelosi rammed health care down our collective throats and lied to us about being able to keep our doctor or health plan. Pelosi's famous words, "If you want to read, it you'll have to wait until we pass it" was in total violation of how Congress is supposed to pass laws. Where was the review period? That's right, there wasn't one. The goal of Obamacare was to eventually end up with a single payer system administered by the government. The Dems wanted to do away with all private insurance companies. This is still there goal today. That's why they push Medicare for all.

Obama was also instrumental in setting race relations back decades. He accomplished this mainly by demonizing the police in two separate cases. The first was Harvard professor Henry Gates Jr. Police received a call that there might be a burglary taking place. Police responded and questioned Gates. Gates had broken into his own house. Because of the nature of the call, the police were following standard procedures. Obama said he didn't know all the facts then went on to say the police had acted stupidly. The truth is his comment was stupid and demonstrated his dislike for the police. The police were doing their job, but Obama took the opportunity to convict the officers of misconduct because the professor, the president's friend, was black.

The second case resulted in the shooting of a black teenager, Michael Brown, by a white police officer. Obama and media again jumped to the conclusion before the investigation had hardly begun. The facts later showed Brown had committed a crime and Officer Darren Wilson had attempted to stop and question him. A struggle took place with Brown attempting to take the officer's weapon from him. The end results were a dead black teenager. Obama and his attorney general encouraged the myth that white police purposely seek out blacks and Latinos as the reason for Brown's death—with the media stoking the flames instead of reporting facts.

On a third occasion, George Zimmerman, acting as a neighborhood watch person in his apartment complex, suspected a young black man (Trevon Martin) was up to no good. His confrontation and a subsequent altercation resulted in Martin's death. Zimmerman was later exonerated as having acted in self-defense. Writing for CNN Abigail Thernstrom said, "President Obama's interference in a local law enforcement matter was unprecedented and inappropriate, and he comes away from the case looking badly tarnished by his poor judgment." Here again, Obama can't seem to help himself when he perceives there's an opportunity to malign law enforcement or the legal system where blacks are involved.

In all three cases, Obama couldn't wait to make derogatory comments about the police and how they handled things. He never bothered to wait for the facts before leaping to judgment. Likewise, the media followed suit as bashing police seems to always fit their agenda. Neither group care about reporting or responding to the facts. The only thing the media and leftist politicians care about is maligning and misleading the story, especially when it involves the police and blacks.

Then we have the case of Dinesh D'Souza, an Indian American political commentator, director, and filmmaker, who was imprisoned for campaign finance fraud after publishing his movie entitled, *2016: Obama's America*. The film covers much of Obama's life; his father's anti-colonialist views; his mentor Frank Marshal Davis, a devoted Communist; Bill Ayers, a leader in the domestic terror group The Weather Underground and Roberto Unger, a Brazilian socialist who was kicked out of Brazil because his socialist views were too radical. These are but a few of the people who helped create Obama's anti-American views.

One of the striking aspects of the movie and facts about Obama's views regarding the USA was proposed in an article he wrote. In it, he says,

> The power of the state must be used to control and regulate private industry, and there should be very high tax rates. They can be taxed up to 100% of their income, as long as they receive a benefit from it. So many countries around the world are growing three to five times the rate of the US as they embrace the American recipe that America is failing at.

How does Obama do it? He embraces an anti-American third worldview, and yet was the president.

It seems Obama and his cronies were not happy with D'Souza and were able to find enough dirt in the campaign fraud area to get him convicted and sent to prison. D'Souza was later pardoned by President Trump. This is just another example of who Democrats go after—anyone who opposes them. Remember Brett Kavanaugh? He was only a Trump appointee to the Supreme Court, and they tried everything they could to destroy him.

Also during the Obama reign was a scandal that became known as Operation Fast and Furious. Working out of the Phoenix office, agents of the Bureau of Alcohol, Tobacco, Firearms, and Explosives (ATF), instructed gun store owners in 2009 to allow illegal gun sales, known as "straw purchases." The gist of the operation was to track the movement of these weapons across the border to the cartels in Mexico. The reality was a concerted effort on the part of the Obama administration, managed by Eric Holder, the attorney general, to develop a story that would inflame American's sensitivities to assault weapons so legislation could be passed to eliminate their sale or significantly reduce their numbers.

Nearly two thousand of these assault-style rifles made it across the border until an insider with the ATF blew the whistle. Obama had planned on highlighting the problem during a visit with Mexico's president. Sadly, these illegally acquired guns resulted in the deaths of Terry Dale, a US Border Patrol agent in Arizona, and Jaime Zapata, a federal agent working in Mexico. Both Holder and Obama said they had no knowledge of the operation at its beginning. It was shown that Holder became aware of it in 2011.

What is truly sad about this whole sordid affair was two Americans had to die before the ill-fated effort on the part of the Obama administration was uncovered to be the farce it was. So desperate were the Democrats under Obama and Holder that they had to create a false operation to show gun purchases in another negative light that would give them the media push to gain US citizen support for creating new and more restrictive gun laws. As congressional hearing heated up and requests for various documents was made of the Obama administration, the president asserted executive privilege in order to keep the documents out of the hands of the Republican-controlled Congress. Those documents have still not been released. The request is hung up in the federal courts. One has to wonder what Obama and Holder have been working so hard to hide.

More recently, a newcomer to the political left has come onto the stage. Robert Francis O'Rourke was given the nickname of Beto by his father, the county judge in El Paso, Texas. His father was very upfront about the reason he did this, saying it would help him politically with Hispanics in the future. Because he's from El Paso, Texas, this maneuver has aided him in becoming popular with the Hispanic community and in being a three-term congressman from that area.

O'Rourke is an Irish American. There is nothing Hispanic about him. In the 1998 time frame, he was driving at a high rate of speed when he lost control of his car. Police reports tell us he attempted to leave the scene, which he denied. A breath test showed him to be over the legal limit, thus DWI. He was also arrested for breaking and entering while in college. He's a leftist politician who has shown he has no honor or integrity. He's willing to do or say whatever it takes to win votes.

Likewise Ocasio-Cortez has no problem telling her own whoppers as well. During a recent trip border at El Paso, Texas she said detainees were made to drink water out of toilets, among other things. In an oped piece by Newt Gingrich entitled, "The Cruel Dishonesty of Alexandria Ocasio-Cortez" he points out the that it took this situation to help him understand how truly "vicisous, cruel and profoundly dishonest she is." I'll address her and others like her—the millennial crowd—towards the end of the book.

I actually like it when both AOC and O'Rourke speak in public or send out tweets, or in AOC's case put out some video. Every time they do it's apparent what kind of idiots they both are. For those of us who pay attention and listen to what they say and how they say it, they are conservative's best hope for the 2020 elections. Why you ask? Because the more people listen to what liberals like these two say, the more the voters will realize voting for people like this will eventually sound the death knell for this country.

The Democrats have two sets of rules. One they apply to others, and a second set they use for themselves. The mainstream media is loath to point out the glaring hypocrisies that exist because they are equally complicit. Democrats serving in Congress do everything in their power to keep the truth from coming to the light of day. With the help of the deep state, a fifth element I've previously mentioned, functioning under the surface in Washington DC, these leftists have been able to lie, hide or obfuscate the truth, or just plain destroy it at every opportunity.

Now that William Barr is the new attorney general, it seems the left is starting to sweat. I make that comment because of how hard they are trying to discredit him. I feel it's just a question of time before the truth will be brought forth and we'll see all the dirt and under-the-table cheating and lying the Democrats have been engaged in since the pre-2016 election season.

We are learning more and more about the Obama justice department and senior members of the FBI who used their political bias to target Trump and work collectively to destroy him. When the whole truth finally sees the light of day, it will really be interesting to see how the Dems try and spin things. Those of us who watch them and are familiar with their dirty tricks and politics will know the truth. Most of us have for some time.

Barr was first hailed as an excellent choice for the attorney general's job when he was nominated. All of a sudden, the left is working overtime to malign and discredit him. Why? Could it be they fear he will uncover the rock where they've hidden the truth in the underhanded planning, conduct, and conspiracy against Trump they've been involved with? Could it be they fear people will end up seeing them for the liars and crooks they truly are? I am one American who is waiting patiently for the truth to finally find the light of day.

The State of Today's Democratic Party

O'Rourke, like Ocasio-Cortez, Kamala Harris, Elizabeth Warren (a.k.a. Pocahontas) and other socialist's politicians are showing us who they really are. They are people with no moral compass, willing to kill the unborn or even being okay with killing babies after birth because they feel that's a mother's right. They are hypocrites of the first order constantly suborning a double standard in our legal system, one for them and their buddies (like the Clintons) and another for those of us on the other side of the aisle. They are people who want to create a big all-controlling government that will tell us all how to live our lives. What we can and cannot do.

With the Green program, laid out by Ocasio-Cortez (AOC), we finally see what the establishment Democrats have long tried to keep from the light of day. They support open borders. They support lowering the age to vote from twenty-one to eighteen. They also support allowing all felons and illegal aliens the right to vote. Bernie Sanders got behind that one recently. Why, you say, are they supporting this? It's simple. They want to add to the voting roles in this country as many people as possible who will vote for them. If they can stack the deck enough, they'll never lose another election and have dominance over our political system and government for decades. Of course that would have to be in conjunction with eliminating the Electoral College.

They support allowing illegal criminal aliens to run rampant in our country, victimizing our citizens protected by sanctuaries. When

Trump suggested he was going to start dropping of illegals in sanctuary cities leftists city, and state leaders went off the rails. Up until this point, these liberals were the champions who are supporting illegal aliens by standing up against the federal government in violation of federal law. Now they are completely against these illegal aliens being dropped off in their cities at all. Trump's move has shown these leftist idiots for exactly who they are. On one hand, they don't mind breaking federal laws and protecting criminals. On the other hand, they don't want the new ones who've recently arrived to become part of their populace. Amazing!

Remember, they want to give everyone free health care, free education, free housing, and a guaranteed income whether a person is willing to work or not. AOC also wants to tear down or refurbish *every* building in American in order to make them more efficient. She wants to build a fast railroad system that will virtually eliminate the need for cars and air travel. REALLY! Where the hell is all this money going to come from? Their standard answer is by taxing the rich. To this date, they have not been able to present logical, concrete proof of how they would pay for such extravagant spending.

Having said this, I recently watched a documentary entitled *The Brains behind Alexandria Ocasio-Cortez*. It was truly eye-opening. You can view this for yourself on YouTube. I now have a better understanding of what's going on. She is a puppet. She's being manipulated by others who have a single goal of taking over the Democratic Party. In their minds, the Dems are not liberal or socialist enough. They are also very anti-colonialists. They see America as the problem, not the cure. Watch the documentary—please.

Then there's the newly elected representatives from Minnesota and Michigan respectively: Omar Ilham and Rashida Tlaib. Omar represents all of Minneapolis and some of the suburbs. A Somali by birth, she is a hard-line Muslim. Her recent comments have shown her to be anti-Jewish. She made comments about 911 referring to the terrorist as "people who did something," downplaying the fact they were Muslims who killed thousands of people. She has proven herself to be disrespectful and unrepentant. I'm sure there are many who she represents who are having more than second thoughts about having elected her. Especially now that research has revealed Omar may have married her brother Ahmed Nur Said Elmi in order to aid Elmi in obtaining citizenship. Elmi's name follows the Somali custom of being named after his father, which is the same name as her father. While being legally married to Elmi, Omar has publicly identified Ahmed Hirsi as her cultural husband and father of her children. Omar released a statement saying, "I have yet to legally divorce Ahmed Nur Said Elmi, but am in the process of doing so." Several months later she filed for divorce.

Then we have Rashida Tlaib, who recently made comments saying the Holocaust gives her a calming feeling. Tlaib is a Palestinian American who represents the west side of Detroit and some of its western suburbs. She is another Muslim who, based on her commentary about Israel, shares the same feelings her fellow member of the house, Omar, does. Both are anti-Semites who are members of the Democratic Party. This is the same party that has been demonstrating an anti-Jewish attitude in both actions and words. Yet here again we find in these two women the face of the Democratic Party. They are not people who believe in being inclusive and representing all Americans.

People like Ocasio have never lived in the real world. She's a twenty-nine-year-old bartender and waitress who auditioned for a part. She's following the guidance and instructions of her puppeteers and is putting the liberal agenda up front and in your face more than anyone previously. Not even crazy Bernie Sanders can top that. And he's been around spewing his socialist bilge for years. The only difference now is he doesn't refer to millionaires, only billionaires.

One of the key liberals in today's society, who best epitomizes and sums up how the elitist on the left see the rest of us, is Bill Maher. On one of his recent shows, he made this statement: "We have a problem in America called spatial geographic inequality, which means that the most affluent and educated people are clustered in just a few cities. We have orchestras and theaters districts and world-class shopping. We have Chef Wolfgang Puck, they have Chef Boyardee. Maybe that has something to do with why Trump voters are obsessed with owning the libs. Because the libs own everything else. While

Americans living in 'blue parts' of the country are having a big prosperity party, those living in 'red states' feel like their invitation got lost in the mail," Maher said. "The flyover states have become the passed-over states. That's why red-state voters are so pissed off. They don't hate us. They want to be us. They want to go to the party." The man's narcissism and arrogance have no limits. He is the true face of elitist liberalism in America.

I have to admit I love it when arrogant narcissistic idiots like Maher and other politicians like O'Rourke, Pelosi, Waters, Feinstein, Ilham, Nadler, Schiff, and Ocasio-Cortez (to mention a few from the long list) open their mouths. They end up showing the rest of America who they really are, what they want to do to our country, and what they think about us. How many remember actor Alec Baldwin referring to Trump supporters as those stinky Walmart people?

Something else I find interesting is how so many presidential hopefuls are flocking to New York City to seek the blessing of Al Sharpton. This is a guy who has less credibility than whale dung. Let me refresh your memories, or in the case of those who have never known the real Al Sharpton, this will be an education into the background of a first-class race-baiting hustler.

There are six different cases where Sharpton has taken to the public stage, pushing the race issue. There was the Bernhard Goetz case in 1984. Goetz defended himself against four young blacks in a subway car after they asked him for $5 by shooting them with a .38. Several of them were carrying sharpened screwdrivers. Goetz was later acquitted. Sharpton demanded that the racist serve jail time.

In 1987, a young fifteen-year-old black girl accused four white men of raping her. Sharpton and two lawyers, C. Vernon Mason and Alton Maddox, functioned as her handlers and fomented protests and chaos for weeks. When the facts came out, it was shown the girl, Tawana Brawley, had lied. One of the men accused, prosecutor Steven Pagones, successfully sued Sharpton, Brawley, and the two lawyers for defamation and won.

In 1990, Sharpton joined fellow radical activist Sonny Carson in leading protests and boycotts against a Korean-owned grocery in Brooklyn. During the boycott, a black teen smashed the skull of a Vietnamese resident with a clawhammer, and his accomplices chanted, "Korean, go home."

In 1991, a Chasidic Jew accidently killed a young black child in a car accident. Sharpton seized the moment by fanning the fires during the funeral in Crown Heights. This resulted in riots with protesters marching, chanting, "No justice, no peace." An estimated 43 civilians and 152 police were injured. At the same time, a rabbinical student was killed by the rioters as they chanted, "Kill the Jew."

There are several other incidents involving Sharpton and the same racist commentary and protesting. One was the Freddy's Fashion Mart situation. Another involved George Zimmerman and Trevon Martin in Florida. Then there was the Michael Brown shooting by a white police officer in Ferguson, Missouri. Sharpton was instrumental in coining slogans like "Pigs in a blanket" or "Hands up, don't shoot" along with others. The end result of his anticop language was reprisal killings of police officer in New York City; Houston, Texas; and in the St. Louis area. All the result of Sharpton and his race-baiting language.

So, now that you have some background on this guy, why are liberal politicians going to him for his blessing? When you know and understand the history of his background and conduct, you know he has zero credibility with most Americans. Sharpton is able to grab media attention because he has the support of many in the black communities around the country. The media loves the controversy he stirs up. It makes no difference to these people that Sharpton's a liar of the first order. Or that he has never once apologized for the harm he's caused during the protests and riots he was directly responsible for. Nope. Liberals do not care what kind of character a person has as long as they can get them votes.

Since the revelation of how they view the abortion issue and being able to kill newborns after delivery, the numbers of people identifying themselves as prochoice as opposed to prolife has changed. Where the prochoice people once outnumber the prolifers, that division is now even. The more Americans begin to see how little the left cares for them, as opposed to illegal criminals, the more the numbers will begin to swing to the right.

Also telling is the fact not one Democrat voted for the biggest tax cut bill we've had in decades. The bill was passed by the Congress-controlled Republican majority. Pelosi, a multimillionaire, dismissed the $1,000 many Americans received as crumbs. What unmitigated arrogance. The Democrats make no effort to hide their desire to roll back the tax cuts and have clearly stated their desires to raise our taxes higher than they were before Trump's tax cut bill passed. Because of the mainstream media's constant efforts to keep the truth from the public, many Americans are truly in the dark. They listen to TV and radio stations that all parrot the same talking points that seek to misdirect the issues and obfuscate the facts.

My hope is the left will continue forward with this conduct and attitude. For the longer they do, the greater the numbers of people who will begin to see their true nature. In the end, the results will be seen in the upcoming 2020 elections.

What's truly sad is where liberal democrats want to take this country. They want a government like Germany's. In Bill O'Reilly's recent article entitled the Plan, he points out what's entailed. Remember the left is always pushing free stuff. They often refer to Europe as examples of how we in American should being running our government.

So, let's just look at Germany for one example. One paragraph from Bill's article says everything you need to know.

> "German workers in Munich pay 8 percent of their income in local taxes. Then Berlin comes in for its piece: 12 percent "health" tax for government run medical care, 19 percent value add tax (VAT) on just about everything you buy, and an income tax that ranges from 14 to 45 percent of your gross wages."

Now it doesn't take a rocket scientist to do the math to realize German worker pay between fifty-three to as much as eighty-four percent of their income in taxes. WOW!! This is where our wonderful socialist liberal politicians want to take our country. Because of the stifling taxes German's can hardly manage to save after paying their regular bills. They have no hope of getting ahead because they're so focused on just getting by. Is that where we as a country want to go?

What's also clear to me is the difference in priorities between conservatives and liberals. Those on the right want to protect our country and its borders. The left wants open boarders so anyone from any country can come in regardless of their intentions.

The right wants a country run by the rule of law. The left follows the law when it's convenient for them. Examples of this are their protection of illegal aliens in sanctuary cities. Or their city leaders warning illegal's the feds are coming for them when they become aware of pending raids.

The conservatives of our country want to help our citizens who need health, or housing to attain those things. Liberals don't care about their own citizens as show cased in California by the thousands of homeless who are living on the streets. Those locations where these homeless people live are also where they urinate and defecate in the parks and on the sidewalks their citizens used to walk through and enjoy. Liberals are also more interested in giving illegal aliens free health care and welfare while they remain in our country illegally.

All one needs to do is to look at those communities that have been government and run by liberals to see where they will end up taking the rest of this country if they are voted into control of our government. They care more about non-Americans than they do about their own country men and women.

The Hollywood Gang

I would be remiss if I didn't address all the wannabee and actual celebrities in Hollywood. With few exceptions, these people seem to think socialism is the only way to go. They staunchly stand behind the Democrats and take every opportunity to slam Trump and the other conservatives. With the actors like Ed Asner and Sean Penn (to name a few), like their buddy Bernie, praising Castro and his communist nation or piling similar support and adulations on socialists like of the late Hugo Chavez of Venezuela as running a kind of people's paradise, one wonders where they'd be today had they been born in those countries.

Today's Hollywood actors or actresses have little to no true understanding of how the rest of the world lives. Granted, many of them started off on the street, waiting tables or performing other such menial work. But they always looked for that shot at getting into the movies or landing a TV show. While I respect good acting, I want to enjoy their performances, not listen to their anti-American bilge. We get enough political negativity from the media and our elected officials. Why must we also hear it from these people? It appears many of them forgot where they came from before they became rich and famous.

While these people may think playing other characters is challenging and fun, I wonder why they don't try being themselves. Or in hindsight, maybe they are and that's why they have to act like someone else. Either way, they choose to live in play roles while other hardworking Americans bust their collective butts trying to earn a living in the real world. The last thing people like them (the working men and women of our country), and I include myself amongst these folks, need to hear is some egotistical spoiled brat actor or comedian complaining about someone like Trump who has done more to improve our country and its economy that any president since Ronald Reagan.

These are also people who are minimally educated. Most are high school graduates, with the exception of Jennifer Lawrence, who dropped out. Or Susan Sarandon who actually has a college degree. These are also people whose egos are so fragile they use drugs and/or alcohol to escape their woes when things aren't going well. This has resulted in many deaths due to over dose.

Like many Americans, I choose to support things and people I like with my wallet. Since hearing people like

Jennifer Lawrence	George Clooney
Whoopee Goldberg	Alec Baldwin
Joy Behar	Jim Carey
Susan Sarandon	Liam Neeson
Meryl Streep	Samuel L. Jackson
Arnold Schwarzenegger	Tom Hanks
Stephen King	Robert De Niro
John Legend	Johnny Depp
Jack Black	Leonardo Di Caprio
Sarah Silverman	Brad Pitt
Michelle Wolf	Cher
Samantha Bee	Barbra Streisand
Ben Stiller	Alyssa Milano
J. K. Rowling	

(It's a long list), I've chosen to turn them off. When these people began putting forth their leftist views, I ceased paying to see their movies. I enjoyed their acting. I will not support their anti-American and anti-conservative views. They are clearly entitled to their opinions, just as I am entitled to turn them off and not spend a dime in their support.

Many of these Hollywood personalities may be Americans by birth, but they are not patriots. Their comments and conduct toward this country have been on display for all to see. For them, like their buddies in the Democratic Party and the mainstream media, Trump has also been the focus of their hate and disrespect. These are not the kind of people who would serve their country in the event of a war. They'd run to Canada where they could find sanctuary.

They are also part of the elite group who see themselves above everyone else. The recent scheme they've used to lie and falsify college records and other entrance paperwork and exams for the kids is truly telling. Like their buddies in Washington DC, they maintain a double standard. One set of rules for us and another for the upper class of our society. wow. Such blatant arrogance. Hopefully, they'll all be held accountable. We're long past due for some of these people to see real jail time.

Then there are all the award shows they have that allow them to parade themselves before the cameras. What a group of egotistical prima donnas. It matters not whether it is the Oscars, the Golden Globe Awards, the Emmy Awards, the Critics' Choice Awards, Gotham Independent Film Awards, the People's Choice Awards, the Grammy Awards, and on and on—it's all about them patting each other on the back. It's about self-aggrandizement. It's about feeding each other's egos and seeing which woman can out dress the other. They live to put themselves on display and pander to their fan clubs. But when their popularity ebbs, they become depressed and become alcoholics and/or drug addicts.

The media holds their events for the same reason. The most recent one was the White House Correspondents Dinner. Because Trump doesn't care for the fake news folks, he chose not to attend. I found their childish reaction to that very funny. These are pundits and so-called reporters who make millions (annual salaries: Rachel Maddow $7M, Chris Cuomo $2.5M, Anderson Cooper $11M, Brian Williams 10M, Diane Sawyer $12M, and Matt Lauer $25M) and live in the big cities, claiming to know how we feel and what we think. Right. They are part and parcel of the same group of narcissistic elitist who want unfettered control of our government and the means of production of this country in order to control us all. Hypocrites, atheists, agnostics, and outright anti-Christians the lot.

You can also look to the Chicago incident involving Jussie Smollett. Based on the information that has come out, this young man fabricated an attack upon himself by paying two other black men, who were extras in the *Empire* series, to perform the task of faking his assault. The evidence is very strong against him. He allegedly thought this hoax would garner him a better place in the show and more money. What it did was show him for the narcissist liar he is. It also demonstrated how he took the opportunity to malign the Trump organization as part of the farce he orchestrated by trying to implicate the president by use of MAGA hats.

Initially, the state's attorney, Kim Fox, allegedly recused herself because of people she knew who were involved with, or friends of Smollett. The Chicago police were loaded for bear and ready to take the case to court when it was summarily dropped. All charges were dismissed, and his records were destroyed. wow, the fix was in. According to sources, the former chief of staff for Michelle Obama had reached out on behalf of Smollett. Here again we find that double standard. The only people with bigger egos and more arrogance that the elitists in Congress are the prima donnas in Hollywood.

Several decades ago, during a time of war, Hollywood had a list of prominent actors who left their careers to fight for their country. While the list is long, I'll make mention of a few:

Charles Bronson
Rock Hudson
Jimmy Stewart
Charlton Heston
Clark Gable
Henry Fonda
Tony Curtis
Sean Connery
George C. Scott
Paul Newman
Lloyd Bridges
Glenn Ford

Lee Ermey
Gene Hackman
Steve McQueen
Ted Williams and Pete
Rose (Baseball)
Clint Eastwood
Elvis Presley
Gene Roddenberry
(*Star Trek*)
Montel Williams
Glenn Miller

This is just a short list of the Hollywood (and a couple of sports) celebrities who fought for our country in time of war. They didn't make excuses or run and hide in Canada. A little googling will result in many more of these true patriots.

I grew up watching many of these people in movies and on TV. We had family TV nights where we watched programs like *Leave It to Beaver* or *Father Knows Best*. There was also the *Ozzie and Harriot* show with their sons David and Ricky. Comedy and variety shows like *Red Skelton* or *Ed Sullivan* were always popular and entertaining. There was no foul language or graphically displayed "blood and guts." These programs were good, wholesome family fun.

Today, you can hardly watch a program on TV or the movies where there isn't outright sexual acts (to include homosexuality) or insinuations on display. The language has become so bad on the big screen and on TV and in music that young people today use the F-word as commonly as older generations said wow. The picture is not a pretty one. The more bad language, immoral conduct, boozing, and smoking they can get into a scene, the more they feel it will sell tickets, not to mention what they're paid by those respective industries.

In addition to this Hollywood has done everything possible to mainline homosexuality. Today there are sitcoms and movies that highlight this life style. While most of mainstream America does not agree with this, the media and Hollywood have done everything they can to make it seem like their life style has been accepted by all. Nothing could be farther from the truth. I'll address this more towards the end of the book.

Hollywood has also gotten into the propaganda business. Movies that portray their concerns over global warming or the evils of big corporations and government help feed their message against these entities. Movies like *The Day the Earth Stood Still*, *Avatar*, or *The Day After Tomorrow*, to mention a few, push their environment agendas. I see their efforts for what they are—propaganda. There are clearly other examples that could be cited covering other areas.

Granted there are a lot of people who are concerned about global warming. I'll be the first to tell you we must protect our planet. Recycling, not littering, ensuring we keep our respective areas (at home and at work) in order are all part of that effort. However, when it comes to believing we, the human race, is capable of destroying our own planet, I think folks need to take a step back and do some deep breathing. Better yet, they need to go back to school and learn something from someone who doesn't have a dog in the race.

Back in the 1970s, these same environmentalist idiots were telling us we were about to enter a new Ice Age. That's right. Another "Ice Age." Everyone was worrying themselves sick of what that would mean to the human race. Now fast-forward a few short decades and its global warming. Really! Scientists have been studying the weather somewhere between 150 to 200 years. They tell us our planet has been around for how many millennia? Now all of a sudden, a handful of scientists are telling us we're destroying the ozone by our carbon emissions. wow. I learned a long time ago one volcano eruption spews out more ozone damages gases than all the engines in the world since they were invented. So how is it now that AOC has determined we only have twelve years until the end of the earth because of what we humans are doing?

Propagandist and liars like Al Gore and Michael Moore have given us movies where they try and show things they want us to believe are true but in reality, are not. Gore's movie *An Inconvenient Truth* showed polar bears resting on chunks of ice. He wanted people to believe this was because the ice was melting, the result of global warming. The truth is polar bears can swim for three to four hundred miles and occasionally take breaks on floating chunks of ice. In another part of his movie, he shows a ship stranded somewhere in Russia because the river dried up due to a lack of water. Here again, the truth was the river had been diverted. It took some time before Gore's movie was called out for all the lies and falsities. In the end, people do get around to finding out who the real BS artists are.

Moore does countless interview using only those that fit his narrative. Both individuals manipulate and manufacture things to prove their distorted positions. They are both liars, propagandists, and people with no honor or integrity. They manipulate their films through the editing process to end up with the message they want us to see. They will do or say anything that will get them a leg up on everyone else. Sadly, they have a lot of followers—people who lack imagination and need to go back to school.

It's also important to note we Americans are not the only people who inhabit this planet. Our liberal environmentalist friends fail to talk about, let alone accept, is the fact that countries like Russia, India, and China produce many times more pollution than we do. Why don't they go to those countries and protest? Oh, that's right. They'd get arrested for disturbing the peace in China. Or put in prison for being a disruptive influence in Russia. No telling what would happen to them in India. Either way you look at it, their environment drum beating about global warming is not really addressing the problem in a holistic effort because they've only focused on the USA.

Before I leave this area devoted to celebrities, I must touch on the professional sports world, specifically the NFL. A couple of years ago, a football player named Colin Kaepernick chose to kneel at the start of a game when the national anthem was being sung and our flag raised. He was protesting the treatment of blacks by white police officers. What he did was disrespect every man and woman who has ever worn the uniform of this great country. As time went by, other, mainly black, athletes followed suit. They too chose to disrespect thousands of our soldiers, sailors, and airmen who lost limbs or died for our and their freedom.

They were protesting an issue that needs to be dealt with in some aspects, but they did it in the wrong way. Whether it was due to ignorance or not, what they did was wrong. Too many people have died to protect the freedoms of this country to be disrespected by people who would probably never consider for a second in putting on that same uniform. It's one thing to be a muscle-bound bad guy on the gridiron, but something completely different when bombs are exploding and bullets are flying. Since that day, I have not watched an NFL game. Because the leadership of the NFL failed to deal with the issue, they are as much to blame. Here, again, I choose to support people and activities I like with my wallet. I know for a fact I'm not the only one in this country who feels the same way.

More recently Megan Rapinoe of the US Women's Soccer Team dropped the F bomb when saying they would not go to the White House if they win the world cup. There was a verbal back and forth between her, her girl friend Sue Bird and the President. Like other liberal athletes, who hate the president, they refuse to be honored by him at the White House. The childish middle school immaturity of these people is disgraceful. Instead of being proud Americans and allowing the president and the rest of the country to honor them at the White House they have to use foul language and put the prejudices against the president of the United States on display for all the world to see. Utterly shameful.

What I'm also discovering about Kaepernick and Rapinoe is their focus on America's past. In a statement by Rapinoe she was quick to evoke the ills of slavery. This is also the real focus of Kaepernick's issues and why he would not stand during the raising of the flag and the playing of our national anthem. They evidently hate what America stands for. To me this is yet another example of what our liberal education system has created in our youth.

California has become a liberal example for all to see when it comes to allowing homelessness and illegal drug use to run unabated. You can't visit Hollywood and other cities in California because they're overrun with these people. The liberal mayors allow them to defecate and urinate in public. Where these people reside, you can't walk by without noticing the stink from the unwashed and the areas where these people have communed with nature. You also can't miss the hypos (syringes) lying everywhere. And California wants us to come there as tourists. Right! This is the liberal paradise where compassion allows people to do what they will with no supervision from the city fathers, law enforcement, or even the citizens themselves. What they see when they drive or walk down those once-famous streets, they've earned. Add to that the growing problem with disease and sickness because of an increasing rat population. Anyone remember the plague that killed tens of thousands in Europe centuries ago. That was the result of rat infestations. There's another reason why my family and I will not be visiting the Golden State anytime soon.

The Second Amendment Battle

The issue of a person's right to keep and bear arms as provided for by our Bill of Rights has been embroiled in heated debates for several decades. For those of us who have studied history the reason is clear. When tyrants control a country and its people, the first thing they do is disarm them. A weaponless citizenry is not a threat. This was one of the primary reasons the Founding Fathers placed this issue as the *Second* Amendment. They saw this as a serious issue that must be protected for all times.

Back in the colonial days, colonist needed weapons to put meat on the table and protect their families from wild animals and Indians. As time went on and more of this country was explored, firearms proved to be valuable tools for food and self-preservation. Liberals know this too. They can't truly control the country via its government if there is an armed citizenry capable of standing up against them. That's why they demonize the NRA and the gun industry. They will never admit what their true goals are. Clear-thinking Americans don't need to be told the true nature of what the liberals are up to regarding our guns. They know.

It is my personal opinion that the socialists/liberals (Democrats) of our country want to incrementally start a process that will eventually leave all Americans defenseless. This will begin by passing seemingly harmless laws that appear to make sense. As the process continues in the Congress, the laws will become more restrictive and punitive. One of the key goals they have is to have every gun registered. That way, they'll know who has what when they are ready to come and take them.

In my forty-six years as a police officer, I've never encountered a law-abiding citizen with or without a license to carry who wasn't a friend to us (cops) and, in a number of cases, was there to assist. It's not the good guy with the gun who is the problem, it's the bad guy with a gun who is.

It amazes me how naïve anti-gun people are regarding criminals. They think by creating or strengthening laws that will keep guns out of the hands of crooks. The bad guys don't play by the rules. They'll buy guns or anything else they want on the black market, steal them, or borrow from another crook. The laws and rules only apply to those of us who willingly obey them. The mainstream media and the politicians know this. But their goal is to disarm all Americans.

Another example of misguided efforts to destroy American's right to keep and bear arms is the aftermath of active-shooter situations. The left takes every opportunity to demonize the firearms industry. They fail to examine who the shooters are. Where did they get the guns they used? What we have found in virtually every case is there were warning signs people failed to see or outright ignored. Many of these killers had emotional or mental problems.

In the Parkland High School shooting, the shooter Nicolas Cruz had been on their radar for a couple of years. The school administration was aware, local law enforcement was as well, even the FBI had looked into Cruz. None of them took him seriously enough, and seventeen people were killed, with another seventeen wounded. Yet the focus was on guns and the National Rifle Association.

Unless and until our society starts taking the issue of dealing with the emotionally and mentally disturbed, serious enough to change the medical privacy laws and policies that fail to allow them to report their concerns to authorities, we will continue to see atrocities like active-shooter killings continue. A good effort is ongoing in many states with "red flag" laws being passed that allow law enforcement, with a court order, to temporarily confiscate a person's firearms until it is shown they are not a threat to themselves or anyone else.

A great example of what happens when a government disarms their population can be found in Australia. When their effort started, they told their people everyone had to register their guns. This was after having already implemented other laws regarding the purchase of a firearm. Didn't make any difference if the gun was for sports, hunting, or collection. All firearms had to be registered. Once this was accomplished, they hit the populace with a new law forbidding any citizen from owning or possessing any type of firearms. Since they'd already gotten everyone to register their weapons, they knew right where to go.

Once the Australian population was disarmed and defenseless, the criminals had a heyday. They could break into any home at any time of the day or night with the knowledge they were the only ones with guns. In one case, the homeowner who had not registered or turned in a gun used it to defend himself and his family. He was arrested because of the gun he possessed. Not sure what if anything happened to the criminals who assaulted them in their own home. Clearly, the Australian government didn't care if their citizens could protect themselves or not. They didn't want anyone armed but those who worked for them (cops, military, etc.)

While liberals yell about people having guns that are not necessary, many of them surround themselves with armed bodyguards. This is just another example of their hypocrisy and double standard. What's good for them is not good for us. The folks on the left fail to heed the research and data that clearly shows us that more guns equal less crime. Criminals don't want to take the chance of committing a crime against someone if that person is armed.

For those who receive one of the National Rifle Association's (NRA) magazines, we know there is always a page entitled "The Armed Citizen." Here you find articles from news outlets across the country describing situations where average citizens protected themselves and their loved ones with a gun. In some cases, they shot their assailant. In other cases, the mere display of the firearm neutralized what could have been a violent situation.

I mentioned in the introduction that I was an NRA supporter. I have been a life member for several years. I am currently at the

"Patron Patriot" level and part of the Golden Eagles. This is a membership I am proud to be a part of because I know this organization fights to maintain our Second Amendment rights against those on the left who want to outright repeal them. Americans need to stand strong in our defense of this right to keep and bear arms. If the left ever manages to disarm us, we'll be helpless and at the mercy of these mental potentates. Just like who you vote for, you're equally responsible for protecting our constitution and its Bill of Rights by ensuring those you elect are originalists (people who steadfastly believe in maintaining these founding works—the Constitution and the Bill of Rights) and will swear to defend and uphold these documents.

Don't forget. Multimillionaires like Blumberg and Soros, coupled with the whole of the mainstream media, want to destroy American's right to keep and bear arms. They don't care about our rights. Guns aren't important to them because they pay guys to carry guns for them. They have bodyguards and protection wherever they go. Average Americans can't afford that. These elitist liberals want to dictate what you and I can and cannot have.

America's Entitlement Mentality

Part of our culture's problems is a belief on the part of many in our society that we are entitled. You hear it in the promises made by politicians. They tell you everyone is entitled to free education, free health care, free housing, a guaranteed income, and on and on. When they're ask how they'll pay for all the free stuff they tell you by raising taxes. If you press them further about how much they'll have to take from people's income they hem and haw and dance around the subject before redirecting you to another area. The reality is they are clueless. They haven't the slightest idea what all their promises entail.

You also hear this in commercials. Whether is a lawyer telling you to call them if you've experienced some type of illness due to the use of some weed killer, or a medication prescribed by a doctor, or because of exposure to asbestos that resulted in mesothelioma. They encourage you to call because you could be rewarded substantial compensation.

Then there are companies like J.G. Wentworth or Peachtree Financial asking you to call them if you have a legal settlement, an inheritance, a lottery winning or some other form of money you're receiving from structured payments. The company's mantra is "it's your money get cash now." They lure you with the possibility of buying that car or boat you've always wanted.

In both cases, the lawyers and the structured settlement financial groups, they focus their efforts at appealing to the greedy nature

of humanity. In most cases these are people who are not well educated and don't have a clear understanding of what is really involved.

Lawyers advertise for people who may have been injured in an
accident with a semi-truck. Or they tell you if you've had a medical
procedure involving a hernia mesh, or hip replacement where such
and such company's prosthetic was used and complications resulted.
They tell the potential client they may be due substantial compensation. A more recent commercial tells the listeners if they served in the
military during a certain period of time and used an ear plug issued
by the military and have suffered hearing loss they should call as they
may receive substantial payment.

What the financial organization or the lawyers don't tell people
is what's involved. In the case of law firms whatever your settlement
is they'll get between thirty to fifty percent of it, plus expenses. The
guys like Wentworth and Peachtree don't tell you how much pen-
nies on the dollar you'll receive by getting lump cash payment from
them when they take over your inheritance, lottery winning, or other
structured type of income. It could be ten or twenty cents on the
dollar. What attracts people to respond to these commercials is the
possibility of getting a large sum of money all at once. They don't
look at the total amount they'll receive over time from their structured payment if they stay the course.

Politicians are no different. They also use catchy phraseology
to appeal to the greed and entitlement mentality of people. As mentioned at the beginning of the chapter they offer free stuff to folks. I
remember the news covering a large black woman in Ohio going on
about how she got herself a "bama phone." Because of the free phone
she was going to vote for him. Politicians make people think the government owes it to them. Nothing could be farther from the truth.

What is clear is the complete level of ignorance of the part of
every American who believes these politicians. There is nothing in the
Declaration of Independence, our Constitution, or the Bill of rights
that makes such a statement. This is the pure fabrication on the part
of politicians who use such verbiage to make the stupid uneducated
people of our country believe they are owed these things.

MICHAEL A. SULLENGER

An **entitlement mentality** is a state of mind in which an individual comes to believe that privileges are instead rights, and that they are to be expected as a matter of course. An entitlement mentality is frequently characterized by the following viewpoints or beliefs:

- A lack of appreciation for the sacrifices of others. Those with an entitlement mentality often criticize the military—failing to acknowledge that it is that selfsame military, and the sacrifices of the countless servicemen who have died in the service of their country, which ensures that they are free to make such criticisms.
- Lack of personal responsibility. Just as those with an entitlement mentality typically expect others to solve their problems, they also refuse to accept that the problems are of their own making. Thus, those with an entitlement mentality are frequently unable or unwilling to acknowledge fault or error; this typically leads to denial. Very prevalent among liberals.
- An inability to accept that actions carry consequences. This can be seen in public schools, where grade inflation and social promotion have resulted in students who expect that they will be promoted to the next grade regardless of their level of effort.
- Arrogantly assuming that privilege reflects on the merits of the individual in question. For example, someone who is fortunate enough to be born extremely intelligent might arrogantly assume that that intelligence is an achievement on his part.
- Increased dependency on Nanny state big government intervention, and an expectation that the government will intervene to solve personal problems. Upon losing a job, for instance, someone with an entitlement mentality is likely to turn to the government for unemployment handouts, rather than immediately seeking another job or training to enhance their skill sets.

- Ignorance of the Bill of Rights. Those with an entitlement mentality frequently imagine so-called "rights" that are in no way guaranteed—for instance, the "right to employment," or the "right to not be offended" or the "right to healthcare". Moreover, they misinterpret the Declaration of Independence's affirmation of their right to *pursue* happiness as a Constitutional *guarantee* of happiness.
- Support for wholesale expansion of Welfare state social programs as a cure-all for perceived "injustice."
- The effort my some to garner reparations for blacks because of slavery. This list is long.

These liberal beliefs are held more by the millennial than the earlier Baby Boomer generation. (Definition from Conservapedia Web page.)

These people have either never been educated about the many sacrifices the pioneers made to just exist, or the sweat and toil of Americans during the Great Depression. Countless thousands of people who live hand to mouth every day of their lives as the country's economy was in the gutter. Why is it that our country has come to this? It is my humble opinion that it is a combination of parents who no longer teach their children about the history of their respective families, coupled with our educational system that no longer instructs students about the true history and struggle of this great nation.

As a Christian in my seventies I was taught by my parents not only the importance of self-determination, but also the importance of taking pride in one's accomplishments in life. Where is the pride in taking handouts for doing nothing? There is no honor in this. Of course those who willingly participate in such endeavors have no real pride or self-worth anyway. Their goal is in getting by any way possible regardless of who pays the bill.

My Christian Perspective

As a Christian, I've been raised to love my fellow man, to be charitable and kind, and to be open-minded. My parents taught us the difference between right and wrong. This was reinforced by our biblical teachings and the guidance provided all of us in the Ten Commandments. Does it frustrate and anger me when I see these people flaunting and making fun of God's law? Of course, it does. I see the Godlessness in places like New York City, San Francisco, Los Angeles, Chicago, Miami, and a host of other large metropolitan cities. These cities have become modern-day Sodom and Gomorrahs. Where possible, I try and speak out against it. I also go to my Lord in prayer and seek His guidance.

I understand why people on the left dismiss Christianity and cast dispersions on Judaism. They rarely say anything against other religions, especially Islam. The majority of these religions (Muslim, Hindu, Buddhist, Judaism, and so on) teach moral guidelines for proper attitudes and appropriate conduct just like our Christian religion does.

Many on the left don't want anyone telling them how to live. They want to do whatever they please, regardless of whether it's considered moral or not. They apply what is called "moral relativism" to justify their drug abuse and promiscuous sexual conduct and life styles. That means partying all night, getting drunk and/or high on drugs, and sleeping with whomever strikes their fancy at the moment, same sex or not. This is conduct that is clearly against biblical teaching and many parts of the Ten Commandments.

You also have people who profess to be Christians but interpret the Bible to meet their own agenda. This is particularly true with the gay community. The mayor of South Bend, Indiana, is openly gay and married to another man. He is one of the Democrats running for the 2020 presidential nomination. In comments he made on the news the other day, he was asked about his religion. He said he takes it serious because it's important to him. Then he commented that God didn't side with one party or another. He said he was sure God wouldn't be on Trump's side.

After hearing those comments, I wondered how people who are Christians can still support people who clearly violate the teaching of our Bible and the commandments so easily. I've already talked about killing babies and what the Bible says about that. I've commented on what the Bible says about lying, envy and more. There is ample commentary in the Bible on these issues for anyone who is a Christian to know where God stands on all of those issues. Here are some Bible verses that speak directly to this issue of homosexuality.

> *Leviticus 18 and 20: Leviticus contains two well-known statements about homosexual activity: "You shall not lie with a male as with a woman; it is an abomination" (Leviticus 18:22). "If a man lies with a male as with a woman, both of them have committed an abomination; they shall surely be put to death; their blood is upon them" (Leviticus 20:13).*
>
> *Romans 1:26–27: "For this reason God gave them up to dishonorable passions. For their women exchanged natural relations for those that are contrary to nature; and the men likewise gave up natural relations with women and were consumed with passion for one another, men committing shameless acts with men and receiving in themselves the due penalty for their error."*
>
> *1 Corinthians 6:9–10: "Or do you not know that the unrighteous will not inherit the kingdom*

> *of God? Do not be deceived: neither the sexually immoral, nor idolaters, nor adulterers, nor men who practice homosexuality, nor thieves, nor the greedy, nor drunkards, nor revilers, nor swindlers will inherit the kingdom of God."*
>
> *1 Timothy 1:8–10: "The law is not laid down for the just but for the lawless and disobedient, for the ungodly and sinners, for the unholy and profane, for those who strike their fathers and mothers, for murderers, for the sexually immoral, men who practice homosexuality, enslavers, liars, perjurers, and whatever else is contrary to sound doctrine."*

The left can say all they want about whether the practice of homosexuality is okay or not in the sight of God. But the scriptures I've just quoted are clear. Those who don't believe in God won't care. They will continue living their lives of sin unabated. I often wonder what nonbelievers think about as they get older in life and begin contemplating their own deaths. Is that when they start wondering if there really may be a heaven where God reins? Is that when they begin reviewing the life of sin they've been living and thinking about what will happen when they die?

People who are agnostics or atheists don't want to believe in God or anything else they can't touch or see proof of. They fail to understand the importance of faith. They understand the concept of love from a physical standpoint. Yet while they know their parents, spouse, and children (if they have any) loves them, they have no way to prove it. Therefore they must have faith they are loved. They can't see the brain inside their skull so they must have faith that it exists and is there. Those of us who are Christians have been blessed with faith. We've been granted this faith from God. Even though we can't see Him we know He's there, we know He loves us, and He sent Jesus to die and take away our sins.

Simply reviewing the commandments Moses brought down from Mount Sinai provides ample clarification regarding the sins all of us are guilty of in one manner or another. The difference is

Christians acknowledge this. We understand we are, by nature, very sinful. We also understand that is precisely why our Heavenly Father sent His only Son to die on the cross. Jesus suffered and died so we may have forgiveness and everlasting life. Sadly, those on the left don't understand and don't care if they're sinful. As long as they enjoy themselves in the moment, that's all that counts. A fellow veteran once commented that there are no atheists in foxholes. That's a good point. How many times has someone who hasn't professed any faith made a religion comment because of disaster or family tragedy?

In the first commandment, God forbids us to have any other God but Him.

People who do not understand this law make gods out of materialistic things. They worship the idea of being famous, rich, and powerful. Some worship images or pray to false gods or even the devil. They even believe themselves to be gods, in violation of the second commandment.

You can hardly watch the TV, a movie, or listen to the radio or recorded music without hearing people taking the Lord's name in vain (the third commandment).

The majority of Americans in big cities today, as in other locations around the country, fail to hold the Sabbath (Sunday) holy. This is the day we are to rest and come together praising our Lord and Heavenly Father (fourth commandment). Even dedicated Christians fail to uphold this commandment today. How many places do we go after church on Sunday for lunch or dinner? How many businesses are open instead of closed. I'm familiar with only two companies who uphold this amendment. They are Chic-fil-A and Hobby Lobby. There may be others. If so, I'm not familiar with them.

In our society today, the number of children born out of wedlock is staggering. There are countless homes with no fathers to help mothers raise the babies these men sired. How is this honoring your father and mother? Is this what they taught you when you were growing up? Those parents who brought babies into this world were given a solemn duty and responsibility to care for and nurture the child until they were able to go out into the world on their own. This is no longer the case in far too many households throughout

America (fifth commandment). Research has also shown us that it's these homes where the criminals come from who populate our prisons today. The importance of a home with a mother and father cannot be emphasized enough.

In 2017, in the United States, the population was 325,719,178. Of that number 17,284 were murdered (sixth commandment). Here, God tells us that we should not commit murder. I would be remiss if I didn't also mention the tens of thousands of unborn babies that are also killed because the mother got pregnant and didn't want the child. These are women with no moral code or conscience. If they haven't repented for their actions, there will be a reckoning on judgement day.

Adultery has been rampant as well for countless decades, only becoming worse in the past several decades. Young people brag about how many sexual relationships they've had. Married men and women even have agreements with each other to "do their own thing" with whomever. Sometimes, they bring outsiders in to share their beds in lustful orgies. The level of promiscuity and debauchery is rampant (seventh commandment).

Also in the same year (2017), we find theft levels through the roof. According to the United States Uniformed Crime report, there were 319,356 robberies, 5,519,107 thefts, and 773,139 auto thefts were reported (eighth commandment).

The last two commandments deal with "not bearing false witness against thy neighbor." This is a regular occurrence among our politicians and the left on a daily basis. To be sure, this also takes place among people on the right side of the aisle, but not nearly with the zeal the left applies to it (ninth commandment). When I think back to the Clintons, I'd have to say they've made lying into an art form. They've done it for so long and so often it's become pathological.

And lastly, the tenth commandment tells us we're not supposed to *covet* our neighbor's house, his wife, his servants, or anything that is his. Remember that definition earlier in the book? We're supposed to be satisfied with the blessing God gives us. If we want something, we're expected to earn it. Far too many people violate this commandment. They're driven by the need to "keep up with the Jones's." This is evident in the above numbers regarding theft/stealing. It's also what the *politics of envy* is all about.

Over the years, I've come across people who claimed they were Christians who were suffering hard times. The ones I feel are truly Christian are the ones who asked God for help. They ask Him to take the burden from them and help them to get through the challenges and ills they are facing. Then there are the so-called Christians who ask God, "Why are you doing this to me? What have I done to deserve this?" They haven't learned that God places challenges in our paths to bring us closer to Him. He never puts more on our plate than He knows we can handle.

Many politicians quote scripture to give the impression they are believers. Their own actions and words betray them for the liars and sinners they are. First Corinthians chapter 13 verses 4 through 13 helps illustrate this point.

1 Corinthians 13:4–13 (NIV):

> *Love is patient, love is kind. It does not envy, it does not boast, it is not proud. It does not dishonor others, it is not self-seeking, it is not easily angered, it keeps no record of wrongs. Love does not delight in evil but rejoices with the truth. It always protects, always trusts, always hopes, always perseveres.*
>
> *Love never fails. But where there are prophecies, they will cease; where there are tongues, they will be stilled; where there is knowledge, it will pass away. For we know in part and we prophesy in part, but when completeness comes, what is in part disappears. When I was a child, I talked like a child, I thought like a child, I reasoned like a child. When I became a man, I put the ways of childhood behind me. For now we see only a reflection as in a mirror; then we shall see face to face. Now I know in part; then I shall know fully, even as I am fully known.*
>
> *And now these three remain: faith, hope and love. But the greatest of these is love.*

What politicians do you know, on either side of the aisle, who are patient, who do not envy, who are not braggarts, and don't boast how they will give us free things paid for by the government? What politicians do you know who refrain from dishonoring their opponents (Trump at the moment)? What politicians do you know who are not self-seeking or don't anger quickly? Politicians delight in bad (evil) things happening to those they don't like. Here again for liberals, it's Trump. True Christians make every effort to talk the talk and walk the walk. Imposters will use aspects of religion to pull the wool over the eyes of the unsuspecting and uneducated.

When my father drowned, I was lost. I wanted answers from God. What I found within myself was an understanding that the Lord does things for a reason. He puts tests and challenges in our paths to bring us closer to him. The measure of us as Christians is how we deal with those difficulties. How we seek His protection, help, and guidance. But through it all, we must never forget that Jesus Christ is our Savior. He died so we may live. He suffered on the cross in order to wash away our sins. Our job is to never forget that and to be thankful for His great love and affection every day of our lives. Anyone can be saved. All it takes is accepting Jesus Christ as your savior.

John 3:16 tells us, *"For God so loved the world that He gave His only begotten Son, that whoever believes in Him shall have everlasting life."* No greater love has our Heavenly Father than to give up His only Son to die on the cross for us.

I accepted my sinful nature a long time ago. I ask God to strengthen my will and resolve whenever I go to Him in prayer. As I mentioned earlier in the book, I like to sing. God has blessed me with a good voice. At the church I attend, St. Paul's Lutheran in McAllen, Texas, I am part of the song leaders' praise group, and am regularly ask to provide special music. One song that really hit me between the eyes several years ago, that I have mentioned previously, was by Steve Green. It was entitled "I Repent." The first verse of the song goes, "Though your love is in me, it doesn't always win me, when competing with my sin." That verse hits the proverbial nail on the head better than anything else I've heard.

For me battling my sinful nature is a daily fight. I can be driving down the road and blow up because some idiot pulled out in front of me causing me to slow down because they failed to yield right of way. Or the lady who slows down making me wonder what she's doing, only to end up turning into a street of parking lot. As a cop one driver did that while I was in my unmarked unit. I turned on my reds and blues and pulled her over. She was driving a nice Mercedes. After introducing myself I ask her for her driver's license and why she hadn't gotten the option that would have given her the ability to signal her turns. She froze in place and looked at me with the most puzzling expression. All of a sudden her face turned red and she smiles a sheepish smile. I'd made me point.

Part of my sinful nature is my complete lack of patience and tolerance for ignorance and stupidity. Someone does something while I'm driving down the road and my blood pressure goes up. My wife tells me to settle down, otherwise I'll have a heart attack. In most cases I find myself silently asking God to make me more patient and tolerant. I'm still a work in progress in both areas. I know it's because of my weakness as a human being. I continue to ask God's guidance and help in fixing my sinfulness. Not sure there's any hope for me at this point, but my faith is strong and I will ask for God's help until the day I stop breathing.

When I hear the vile and vitriolic commentary and lies by people in the mainstream media whenever they're discussing Trump, I wonder if they will ever realize how ugly and vindictive they sound. The hate that these people display by their own words and actions is the proof that they are Godless and immoral. As a Christian, I am constantly wondering why we all can't just get along. Why can't we agree to disagree and respect each other? Why can't we engage in civil discourse and the sharing of ideas? This would clearly be the nature of our society if we were all students and followers of a religion.

But such thoughts are not feasible because these people are incapable of developing the faith it takes to become a child of God. In today's society, the left has become more militant and vicious towards those they disagree with. Just watch what happens a college campuses across the country. You'll see people who have been invited to speak and represent a conservative point of view threatened with violence and shouted down. You see the college or university administrators turn a blind eye, or passively suborn the conduct. Clearly, fascism is rapidly growing in America.

I leave this chapter with a question. I've lived in the Rio Grande Valley since retiring from the Air Force in June of 1993. Before that, Janie and I lived here several years while I attended college and earned a degree. I've been a member of a traditional Mexican American Catholic family for more than fifty years.

Down here in South Texas, the vast majority of Hispanics are Catholics and Democrats. How can a people so dedicated to their faith and religion tolerate a party that supports and fights for killing babies (abortion before or after birth)? How can you, as good Christians, allow these politicians you vote for to lie and push our country toward socialism (envy and coveting that are both against the Commandments)? How can you tolerate their support of the drug culture and promiscuous sexual deviance? How, as good Christians, can you stand by and watch your elected officials support criminal activities and practices without saying a word? And that's both here in the Valley and in Washington. What you don't condemn, you support. That makes you co-conspirators with those who are actually the Godless ones violating our Lord's teachings and commandants practically every time they get out of bed and open their mouths.

If you are truly Christians, you need to search your hearts. You need to ask God to guide you as you seriously review what the party you support stands for. Look at the people who make up your party and ask yourself, are these people Godly people? If you search your heart and honestly look at how they conduct themselves, the constant lying and denigrating of those they disagree with and how they fail to support those who espouse their Christianity openly, then why do you support them? You need to take a really hard look at yourselves and what's been taking place in your name by the people you've voted for. This is something you cannot confess and get absolution for. No amount of Hail Marys or Our Fathers will give you absolution. That won't happen until you turn away from the sinners you support.

Don't think I'm not including you who are of other denominations or religions in this. This is a job of review and reflection all Christians and people of other faiths must do as well. The bar that these politicians must meet or past is laid out in our respective bibles and scriptures. This means the moral codes of conduct, attitude and treatment of others must meet the expectations of (for Christians) Christ's teachings in the New Testament. Or what's taught in the Hebrew Tora. Or the Muslim's Koran. Likewise in the Buddhist and Shinto religions of the Far East.

Loving thy neighbor as thy self. Being generous with those in need. Being good Samaritans for those who are ill or injured. Not judging the speck in the eye of another lest we fail to see the log in our own. Like Christ said when He admonished the crowd who was preparing to stone Mary Magdalene, *"he who is without sin cast the first stone."* We know no one did. They all realized they were also sinners and had no right to judge. I pray this challenge is met by all who read this book.

Final Thoughts

When I began writing this book, I didn't realize what a walk down memory lane it would be. I was motivated to write this because of the ongoing chaos and mess that has and continues to exist in Washington DC and the American political system as a whole. Like many average folks who don't live in big cities and are focused on making a living in order to feed and care for our families, the non-stop infighting and just plain hatred on display daily has become shameful and unbearable.

Why can't the people we elect to serve and represent us in Congress simply do their jobs? Why is it a few powerful congressmen and women, along with senators, always have to be the ones setting the agenda and cracking the whip to ensure their collective flocks don't stray? For me, the answer is simple. These people are allowed to stay in those positions until they die or voted out of office. The power of the office has corrupted them. Like the old cliché says, "Power corrupts, absolute power corrupts absolutely."

We can't complain directly to any of these politicians. The members of their staff provide a buffer zone between average citizens like you and I. This keeps the true nature about how many Americans feel about their conduct and attitudes away from them. This no doubt results in them falsely thinking they are supported by their electorate. Even if we could really voice our views and frustrations with them, I doubt many of them would care one way or another.

There are no term limits for members of Congress. It's interesting to note that after Franklin D. Roosevelt (FDR) died while serving his fourth term as president, the Congress moved a few years later to pass the Twenty-second Amendment on February 27, 1951. This amendment effectively limits any person elected President of the United States to no more than two terms in office, or no more the ten years. Why did Congress take this action? Did Congress fear a strong popular president like FDR arriving on the political scene at some later time who was as equal to controlling things as he was? One can only speculate. So, as the cliché goes, what's good for the goose is good for the gander.

In discussing term limits for congress, I've heard friend after friend, family member after family member, along with scores of others on social media say it will never happen. Congress will never vote term limits on themselves. They've become too intoxicated with the power and majesty their respective offices give them. But I'm here to tell you to be of good spirit and look to the future for liberation from these megalomaniacs and mini potentates. That future lies within your own hands.

Article V of our Constitution provides the guidelines for amending this great document. It states,

> *The Congress, whenever two thirds of both houses shall deem it necessary, shall propose Amendments to this Constitution, or, on the Application of the legislatures of two thirds of the States, shall call a Convention for proposing Amendments, which, in either case, shall be valid to all Intents and Purposes, as Part of this Constitution, when ratified by the legislatures of three fourths of the several states, or by conventions in three fourths thereof, as the one or the other Mode of Ratification may be proposed by the Congress; Provided that no Amendment which may be made prior to the Year One thousand eight hundred and eight shall in any Manner affect the first and fourth Clauses in the Ninth Section of the first Article; and that no State, without its Consent, shall be deprived of its equal Suffrage in the Senate.*

When Article V referrers to both houses, it means the House of Representative and the Senate. After hearing some of the newly elected members of the Congress speak about our government and how it runs, I realized there are a lot of folks who are really ignorant about their own government. That would be some of the members of the current freshman class. People like AOC and Ilham.

What Article V is saying is there are two ways to amend the Constitution. The first is when two-thirds of both houses propose an amendment, it must be ratified by three-fourths of both houses in order for the amendment to become official.

The second way of amending the Constitution is by application of the legislatures of two-thirds of the States calling for a convention for proposing amendments, that is subsequently ratified by three-fourths of the States, thus bypassing congress altogether.

This is something that will have to be a true grassroots effort on the part of average Americans throughout our great country. People in each state are going to have to grab this bull by the horns in earnest if it ever has a chance of coming to pass.

As long our political system remains controlled by the puppet masters like George Soros, or the brain trust behind Alexandria Ocasio-Cortez, etc., there will be no change and our country will eventually be destroyed from within by these so-called servants of the people.

This is a monumental task because far too many of our citizens are enthralled by the pied piper mysticism of the mainstream media and smooth-talking orators and carnival barkers like O'Rourke, Obama, AOC, and others. Just like the followers of Jim Jones and David Koresh, Americans by the millions will be lead down the primrose path to oblivion. They will believe the pie in the sky promises these charlatans give them. But like the majority of politicians in the past (with few exceptions), once elected, their promises will turn out to be as hollow as their hearts. So far, only Ronald Reagan and Donald Trump have actually been able to fulfill many of the promises they gave us while on the campaign trail.

We as Christians must endeavor to do our parts as well. It won't be easy because we've already allowed ourselves to be made irrelevant by the media and leftist politicians. We've turned the other cheek so many times our collective heads are still spinning. We need to seek guidance through prayer. We need to unite in a common cause in order to preserve this country we all love.

We must all also wake up to the fact that the liberal education system in this country for the past several decades has managed to change the hearts and minds of our younger generations. They don't focus on the history of this great country by looking at the struggle and difficulties our founders and citizens went through during those very tough years. No. They focus on the fact they were slave owners. Or that they took land away from the America Indians. They don't take into consideration that those people lived and grew up in a totally different era and culture. They blame America for all the problems of the world and want to dismantle its history thinking they'll be able to right all the past wrongs based on today's culture and beliefs.

Changing this attitude and way of thinking will not happen anytime soon. As long as the liberals of this country control the educational institutions from kindergarten through high school, along with our colleges and universities, the only way any possible headway can be made is through home schooling and private parochial institutions. My wife and I plan on sending our newest grandsons to Christian schools when the time comes. We want to ensure they are raised as followers of our Lord and Savior Jesus Christ. By doing this we know they'll grow up understanding what's right and wrong based on biblical teachings and the Ten Commandments.

As senior citizens in our seventies Janie and I know are time on earth is growing shorter. We want to ensure our daughters and their husbands are clear on our desires to raise these kids as responsible, well educated, Christian adults. We ask God to guide us in this endeavor regularly in prayer. I pray you will also do the same in your respective families.

We also need to work harder at bring civility back. The hatred and vitriolic language we hear in the media, from our politicians, on display with late night comedians, or displayed in various forms of print must stop. Those of us who are tired of hearing and reading this stuff must turn the channel and stop buying the periodical that supports it. We must make it crystal clear to our elected officials we will vote for someone else if they don't step up and start working for change. Positive change. Not rhetorical lip service. I don't expect this will happen in my lifetime. But I truly hope it will in the not too distant future. For our children's and grandchildren's sakes.

Regardless of what you hear said by the fake news, there are a lot more Christians in this country than they are willing to admit. We must shed the fear of being called out if we let people know how we see things from a Christian's perspective. We must not be afraid to speak out and tell those who would try and silence us that we will no longer be silenced. We must have the moral courage and certainty of our Christian convictions to shout them to the skies. We must do this singularly and collectively. We must also teach our children to follow in our steps as they grow in both their faith and understanding of the problems our great country is facing.

To help illustrate the problem I'm including an e-mail sent to me by John Sorg. John and I have known each other for more than twenty years. We met at Culver when I was the senior counselor for Naval Company Two. The e-mail tells us how a Tennessee high school principle addressed the tradition of praying before football games.

I FIND IT INTERESTING THAT A HIGH SCHOOL
PRINCIPAL CAN SEE THE PROBLEM, BUT OUR SOCIETY
CANNOT.

This is a statement that was read over the PA system at the
football game at Roane County High School, Kingston, Tennessee
by school Principal, Jody McLeod

> "It has always been the custom at Roane County
> High School football games, to say a prayer and
> play the National Anthem, to honor God and
> Country."

> Due to a recent ruling by the Supreme Court,
> I am told that saying a Prayer is a violation of
> Federal Case Law. As I understand the law at
> this time, I can use this public facility to approve
> of sexual perversion and call it "an alternate life
> style," and if someone is offended, that's OK.

> I can use it to condone sexual promiscuity, by
> dispensing condoms and calling it, "safe sex." If
> someone is offended, that's OK.

> I can even use this public facility to present the
> merits of killing an unborn baby as a "viable"
> Means of birth control." If someone is offended,
> no problem...

I can designate a school day as "Earth Day" and involve students in activities to worship religiously and praise the goddess "Mother Earth" and call it "ecology…"

I can use literature, videos and presentations in the classroom that depicts people with strong, traditional Christian convictions as "simple minded" and "ignorant" and call it "enlightenment."

However, if anyone uses this facility to honor GOD and to ask HIM to Bless this event with safety and good sportsmanship, then Federal Case Law is violated.

This appears to be inconsistent at best, and at worst, diabolical. Apparently, we are to be tolerant of everything and anyone, except GOD and HIS Commandments.

Nevertheless, as a school principal, I frequently ask staff and students to abide by rules with which they do not necessarily agree. For me to do otherwise would be inconsistent at best, and at worst, hypocritical. I suffer from that affliction enough unintentionally. I certainly do not need to add an intentional transgression.

For this reason, I shall "Render unto Caesar that which is Caesar's," and refrain from praying at this time.

"However, if you feel inspired to honor, praise and thank GOD and ask HIM, in the name of JESUS, to Bless this event, please feel free to do so. As far as I know, that's not against the law—yet."

One by one, the people in the stands bowed their heads, held hands with one another and began to pray.

They prayed in the stands. They prayed in the team huddles. They prayed at the concession stand and they prayed in the Announcer's Box!

The only place they didn't pray was in the Supreme Court of the United States of America—the Seat of "Justice" in the "one nation, under GOD."

Somehow, Kingston, Tennessee Remembered what so many have forgotten. We are given the Freedom OF Religion, not the Freedom from Religion Praise GOD that HIS remnant remains!

JESUS said, "If you are ashamed of Me before men, then I will be ashamed of you before MY FATHER."

Be ye of good cheer for our Lord and Heavenly Father are with us. May God bless and keep you all in His mercy and grace.

VIA - PD Police Chief, Michael A. Sullenger, May of 2013

About the Author

Michael A. Sullenger is a retired US Air Force Security police, major, and disabled veteran. He is also a retired associate professor, having taught American and Texas Government at the junior college level. He has been involved in the law enforcement career for the past forty-seven years, and currently is the chief of police for an airport police department. Mr. Sullenger speaks three languages and holds a bachelor's degree in criminal justice and a master's in international relations with Middle Eastern studies with a focus on terrorism. He has authored a number of articles on the martial arts and some dealing with his police career field. While teaching at the college he co-authored a portion of the American and Texas Government text and workbook.

Mike and his wife and family lived ten of their twenty years with the military in Europe (Spain, Germany, and England). His two daughters, Erica and Michelle, have given them three grandsons.

CPSIA information can be obtained
at www.ICGtesting.com
Printed in the USA
BVHW082224030120
568544BV00001B/16/P

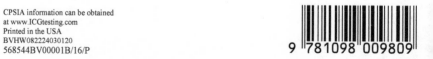